Inspiration From What Is

Also by Catherine Thomas

Awakening the Vulnerable Heart

Inspiration

FROM WHAT IS

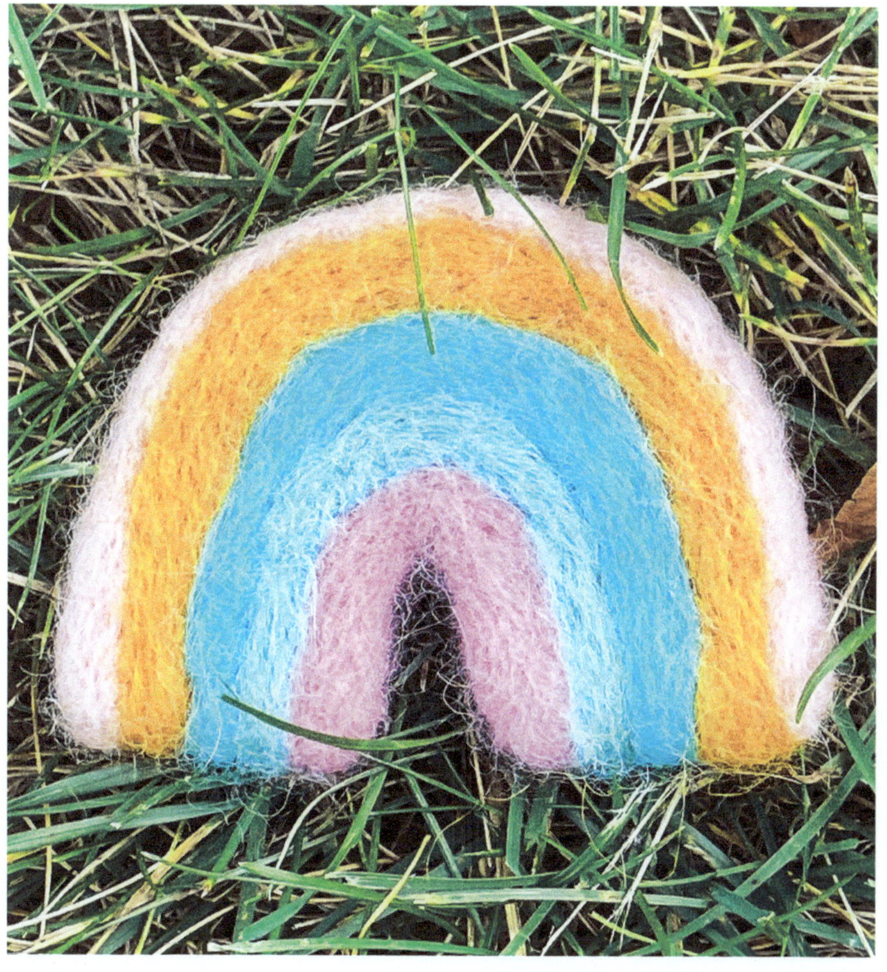

Catherine Thomas

All rights reserved. No part of this publication may be reproduced, distributed, or transmitted in any form by any means, including photocopying, recording, or other electronic methods without the prior written permission of the author, except in the case of brief quotations embodied in reviews and certain other noncommercial uses permitted by copyright law. For permission requests, write to the author at the email address below.

Copyright © 2024 Catherine Thomas

Photographs by Catherine Thomas

Published by Catherine Thomas
Cedarburg, Wisconsin 53012

catherine.thomas.wi@gmail.com

ISBN 979-8-218-46568-1

Library of Congress Control Number: 2024916818

Designed by Tell Tell Poetry

Printed in the United States of America

First Printing, 2024

With much love and infinite gratitude,

I dedicate this collection to the people of Cedarburg,

the community of my heart

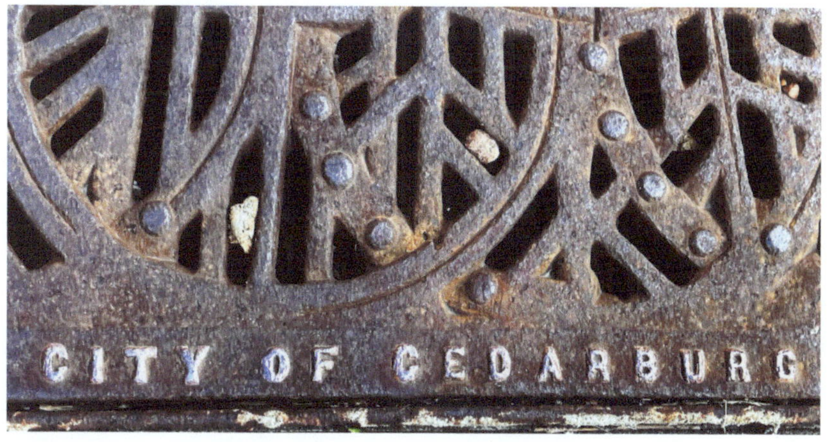

Note About Photos

Apart from *I Don't*, photographs throughout the book were captured, unaltered, during walkabouts.

Contents

What Is

Ensemble Cast

Matters of the Awakened Heart

Self-Possession

Inspiration From What Is

What Is

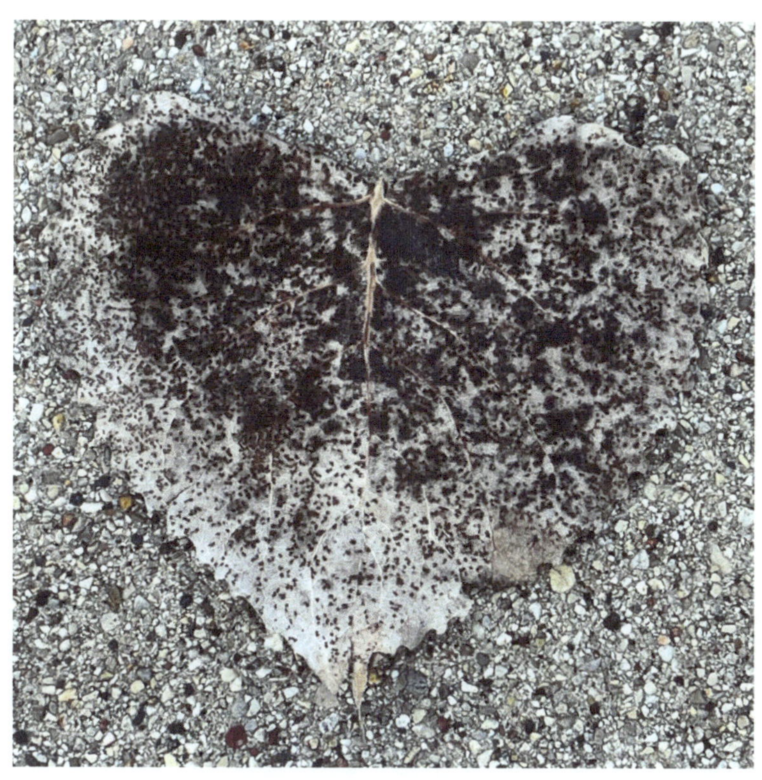

Illumination

In unfathomable times
Those who can
Find the light
Are charged with
Reigniting the wicks
Of those who've
Lost their way.

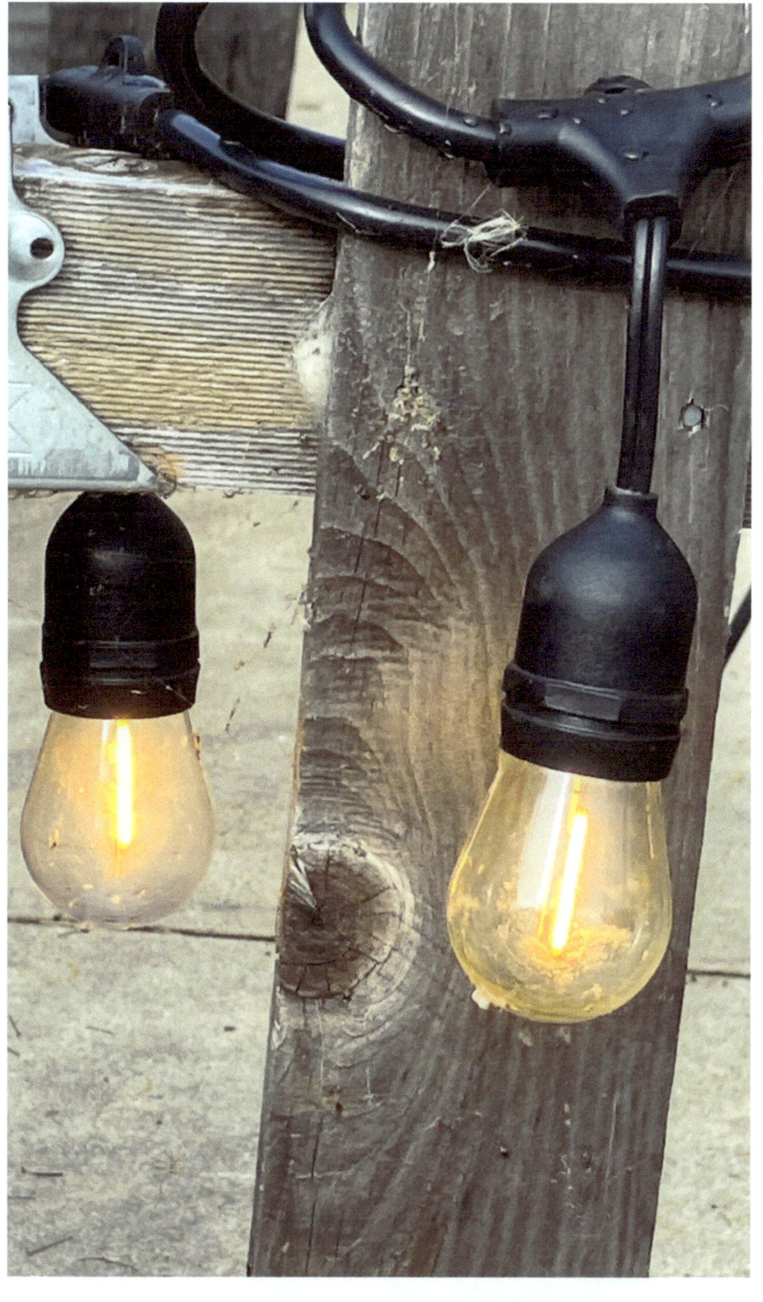

Changing Room

It took
Stripping away
Labels of
Daughter wife mother
To return
To equilibrium
And be me.

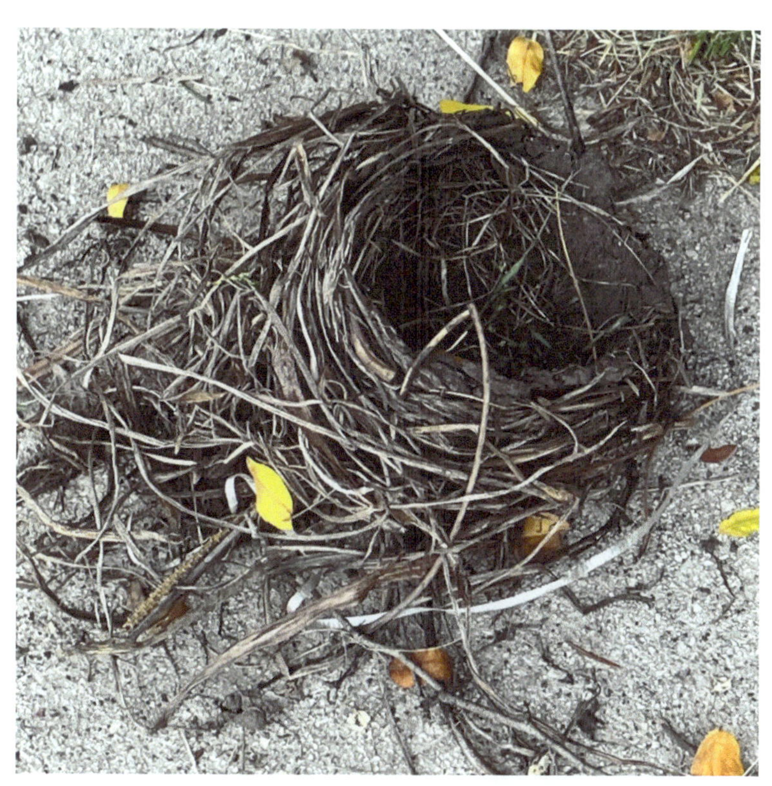

Reintroduction

I accept
What I am
And that
Who I was
No longer is.

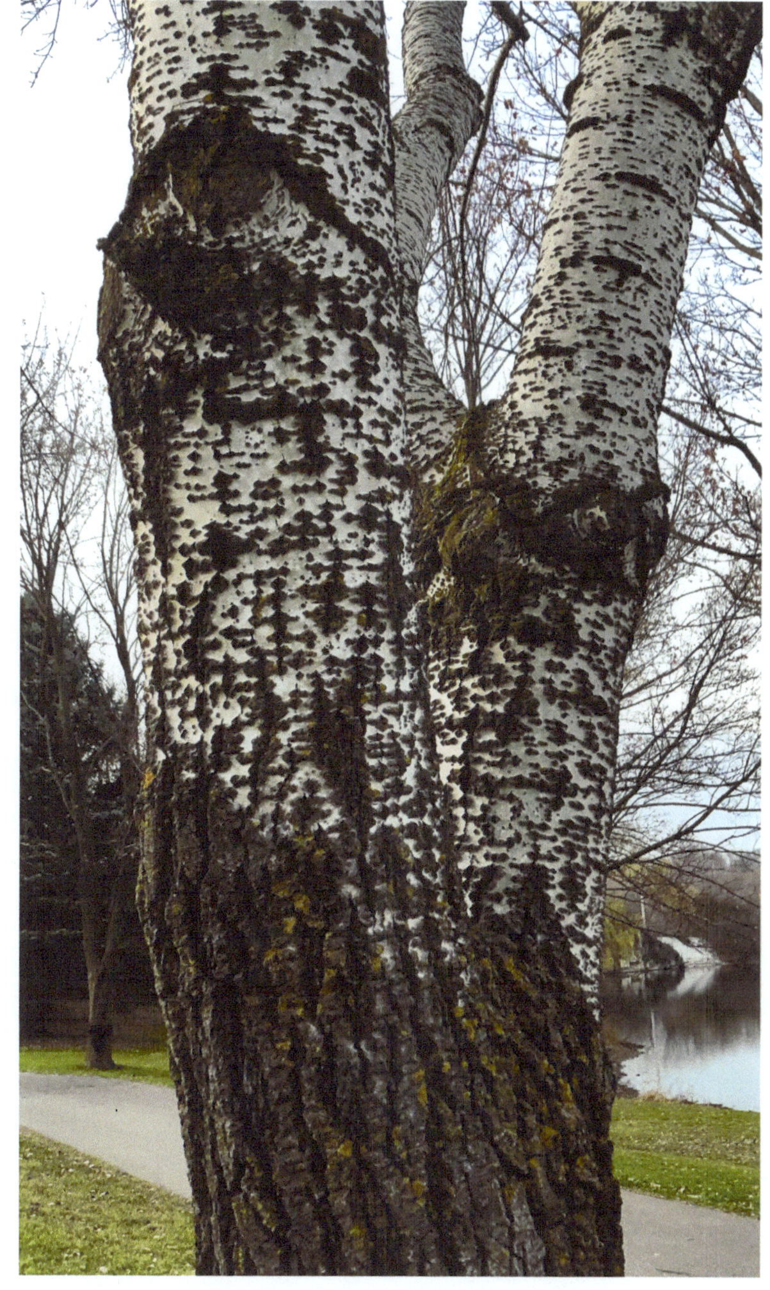

Urban Monk

I live
A life
Of solitude
In plain
Sight.

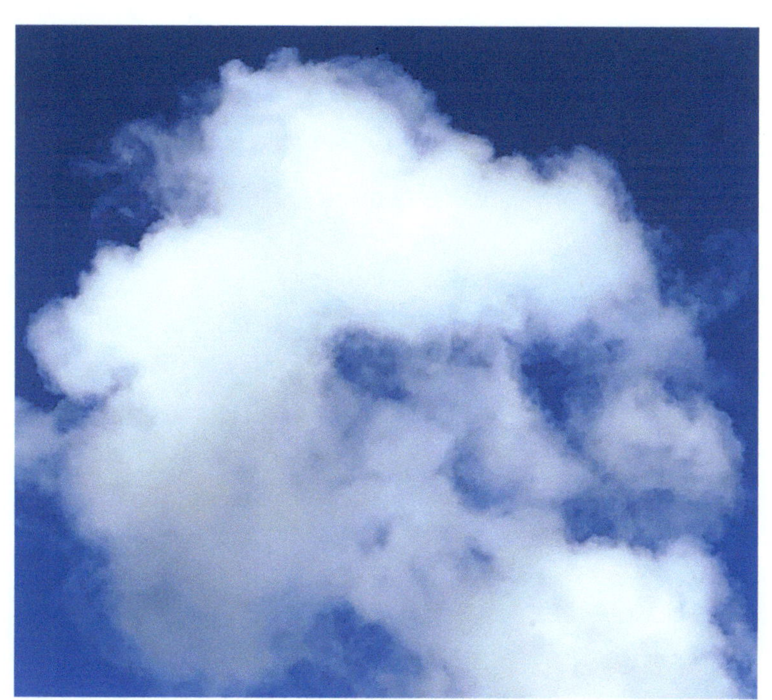

Quietude

Shutting myself off
From the world
Was necessary
To discover
My true mission
Within it.

Agency

Addressing the human needs
Of a spiritual being
Is a true
Act of faith.

Gratitude

I have
What I need
For the life
I have.

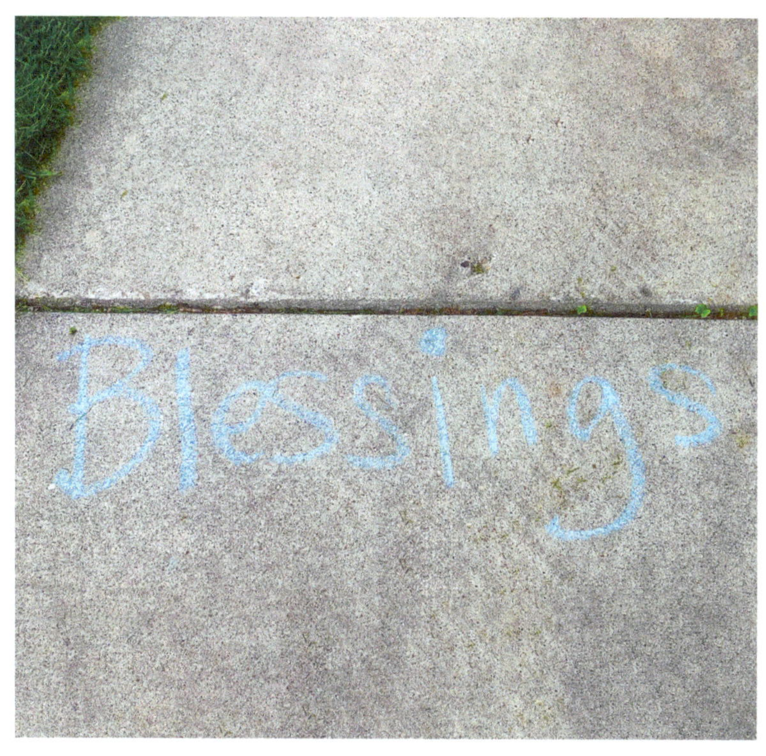
Blessings

Crossing Bridges

In a world
Seemingly spinning
Out of control
We can choose to live
With what we know
Or suffer thoughts
Of outcomes
Derived from unquiet minds.

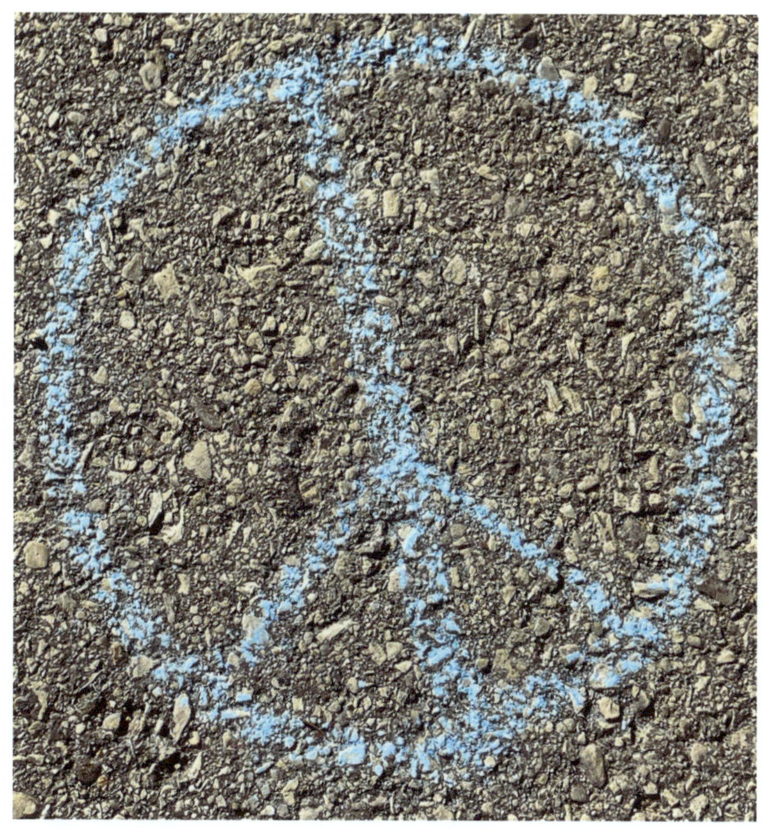

Laser Focus

It's not
That I'm in denial
Of what
Is
It's that
I choose
To shine my spotlight
On what's
True.

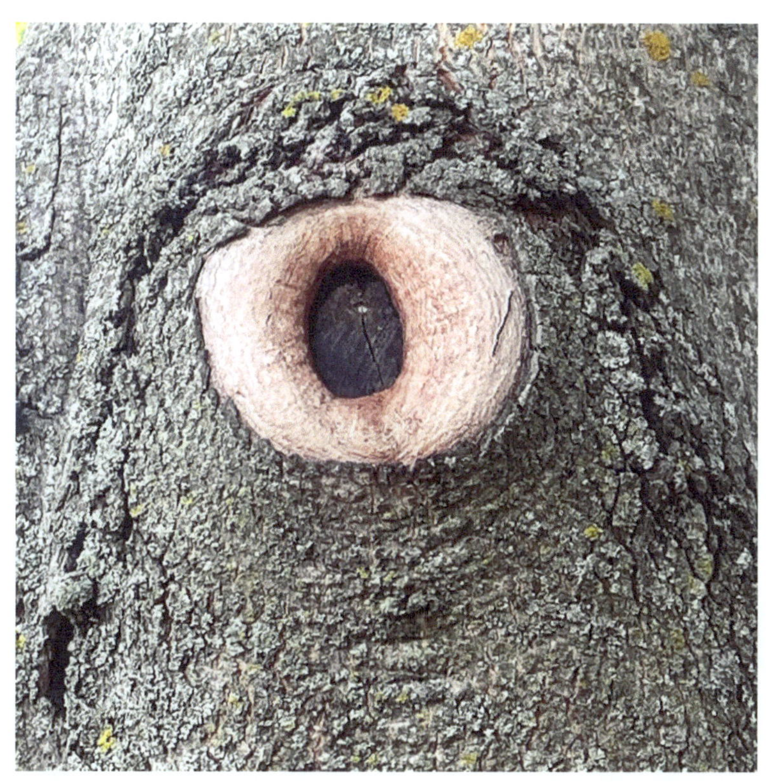

Full Circle

Just because
I now see things
As they truly are
Doesn't mean my heart
Completely abstains
From wishful thinking.

Shifting Gears

Not enough
Used to be
More than enough
Until I finally
Became enough
For myself.

Takeoff

There will come
A glorious day
When you claim
The realized right
To untether yourself
From burdensome constraints
Allowing true self
To take flight.

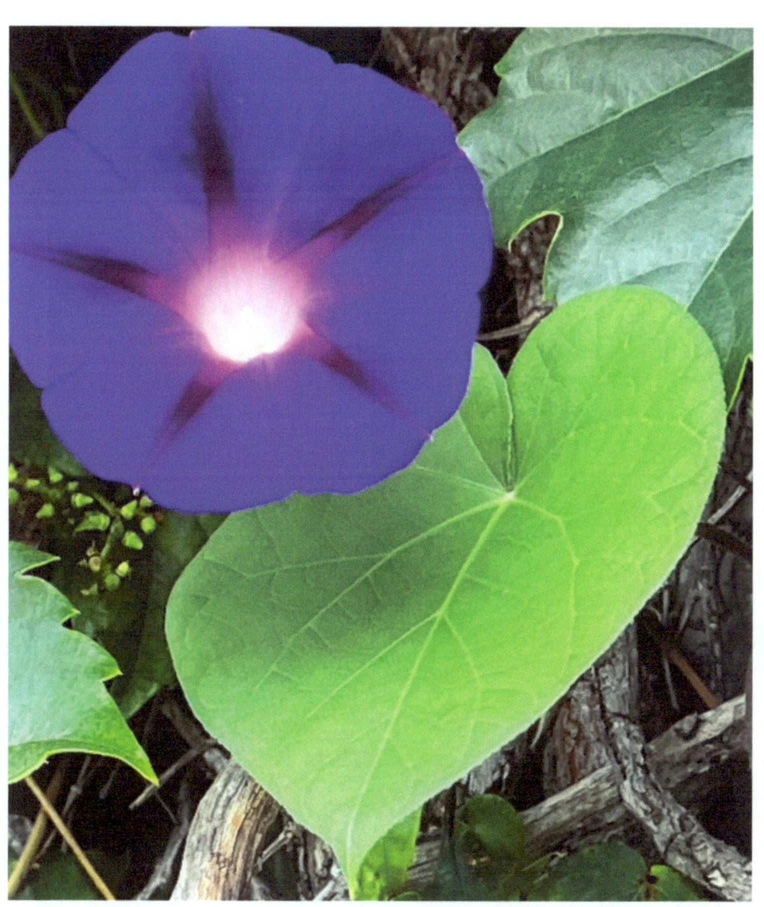

Viewfinder

Just because you're able
To reframe life circumstances
Doesn't guarantee
Everyone else
Sees through a similar lens.

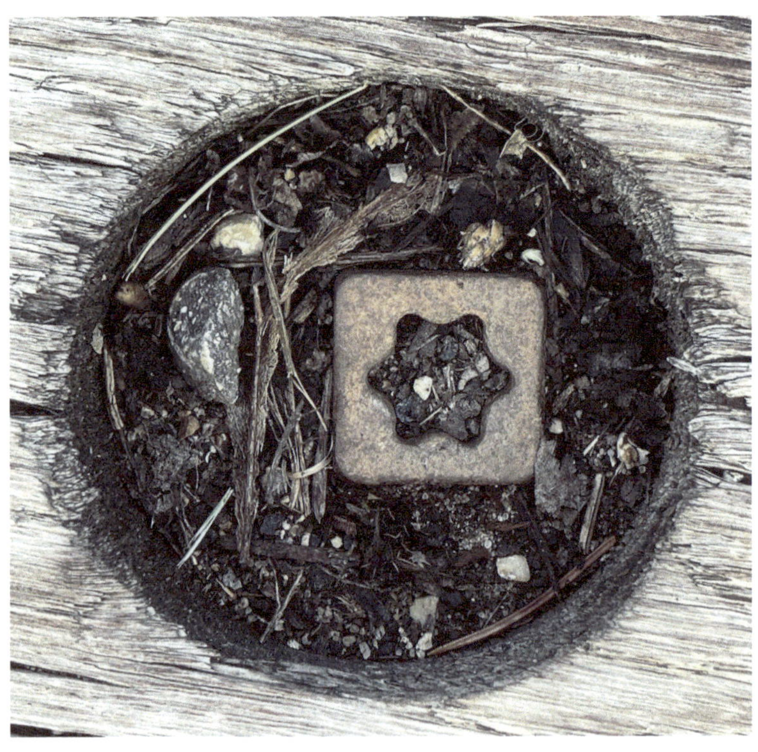

Battle Line

Sometimes
The fiercest warrior
Wants nothing more
Than to lay
Down her sword
And surrender into
Strong and loving
Arms.

Cerulean Skies

When we speak of
Leaving or returning home
Our fallible human nature
Forgets the fact
We're never disconnected
Due to the metronome
That is our heart.

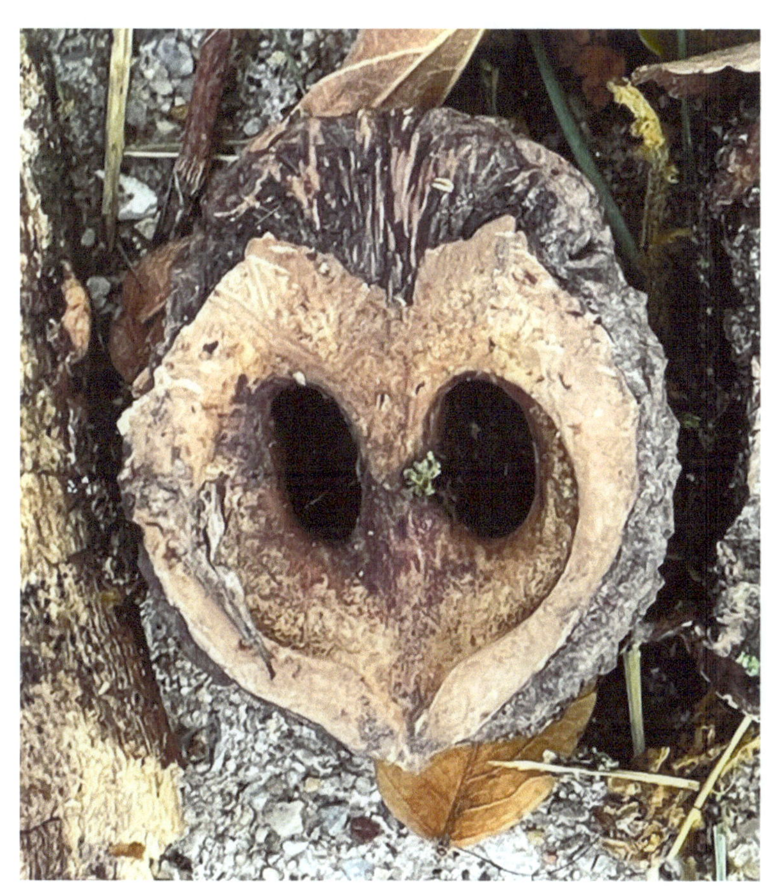

Reason and Season

You kept me afloat
In the deep end
When my feet
Couldn't touch bottom.
Having reached shallow waters
The time has come
To emerge from the pool
Independently.

After Hours

The vulnerable calling
Of the soul
Is often camouflaged
By external turmoil.

Grazing

One opts
To feed
The illusion
Because seeing
Things clearly
Is unpalatable.

Bare

Layer upon layer
Of thorny leaves
Must be removed
To reach the
Artichoke's tender heart.
Casting off
Illusory narratives
Reveals ours.

Undone

The time
Will come
When the most
Resilient flower
Sheds her petals.

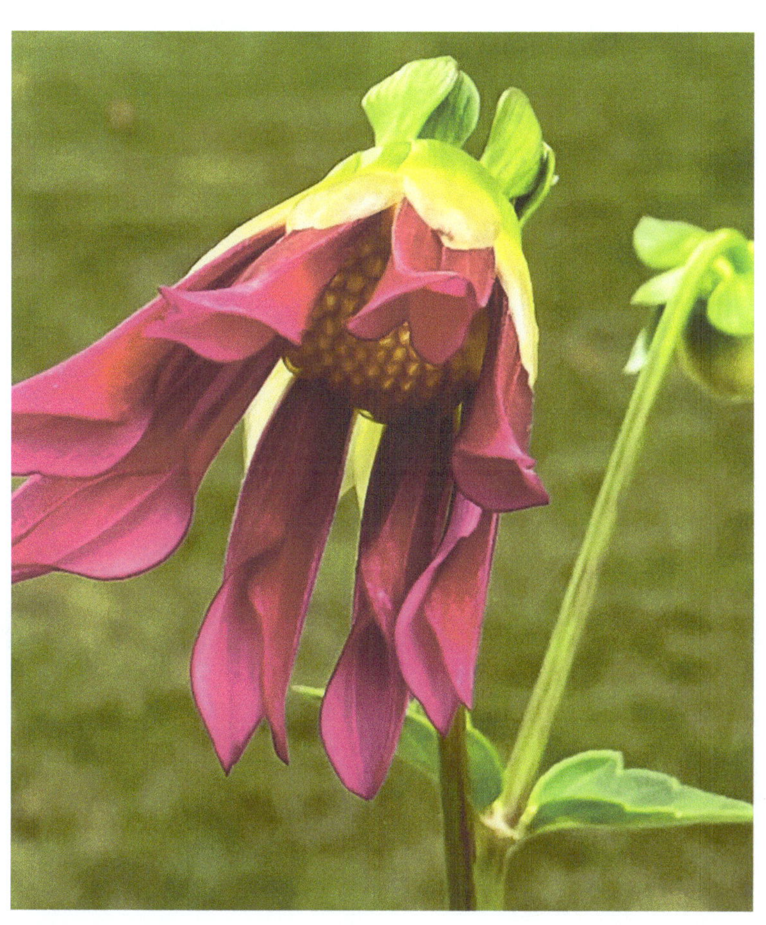

Baited

You can either
Pace ignorance
Desperately signaling
For acknowledgement
Or veer away
Avoiding a collision
With the looming
Brick wall.

Member of the Flock

Even when
You're powerless
To intervene
In unthinkable chaos
Witnessing your cries
Being mirrored
By others
Somehow softens
The devastation.

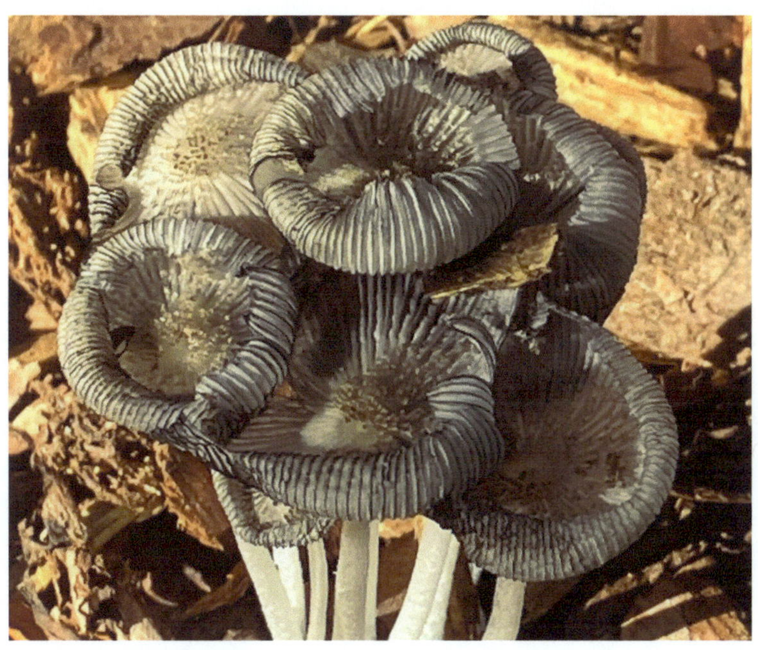

Searching for Signal

Sometimes I wonder
What it means
About humanity
That we've become
Too disconnected
From one another
To answer queries
With hard truths
Rather than silence.

Starting Route

The revolving door
Moves with intention
You are either
In or out.
Pausing indecisively
Between destinations
Results in a standstill
Of body and mind.

Age in Place

The physical body
Prefers the path
Of least resistance
Opting to remain
In familiar surroundings.
It turns a deaf ear
To the soul's plea
Of renouncing
Perceived sanctuary
For the prospect
Of intangible advancement.

Lockdown

When the caged bird
Discovers the door
Has always been open
That creates more disquietude
Than perceived captivity.

Mirror Image

It's only
In a state
Of beautiful stillness
The truth
Can be seen.

Sizing Up

Trying to fit
What was
Into what is
Is akin
To trying on the shoes
You took your first steps in
And being surprised
They've been outgrown.

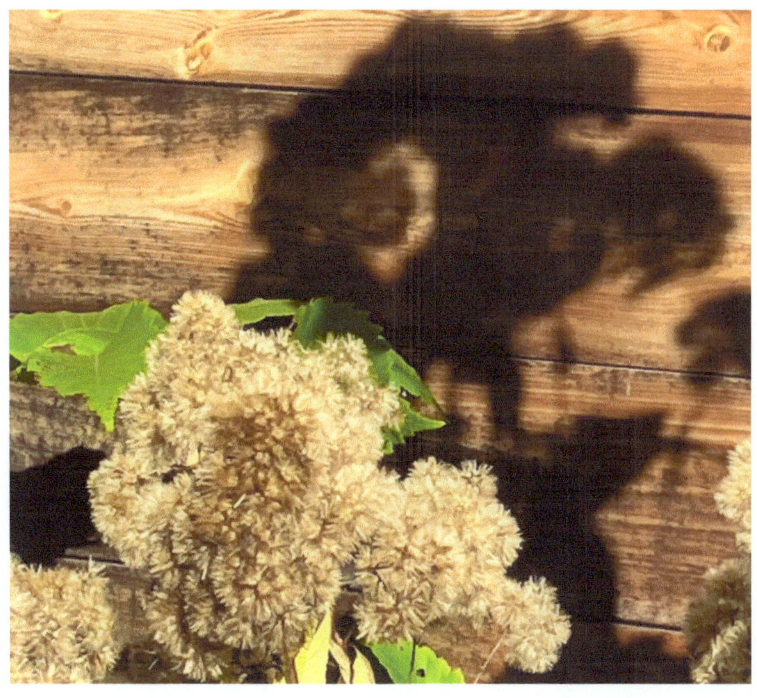

Skim Coat

When gaping holes
Expand faster
Than restorative compound
Can remedy
It's time to cease
Fixing the unfixable.

Clean House

Choosing to leave
The existing wallpaper
On a singular surface
After reenvisioning
The entire abode
Negates the ability
To entertain
A fresh perspective.

Savior of Self

Looking to others
To restore wholeness
Brings the same despondency
As attempting to return
Airborne dandelion seeds
To their stem.

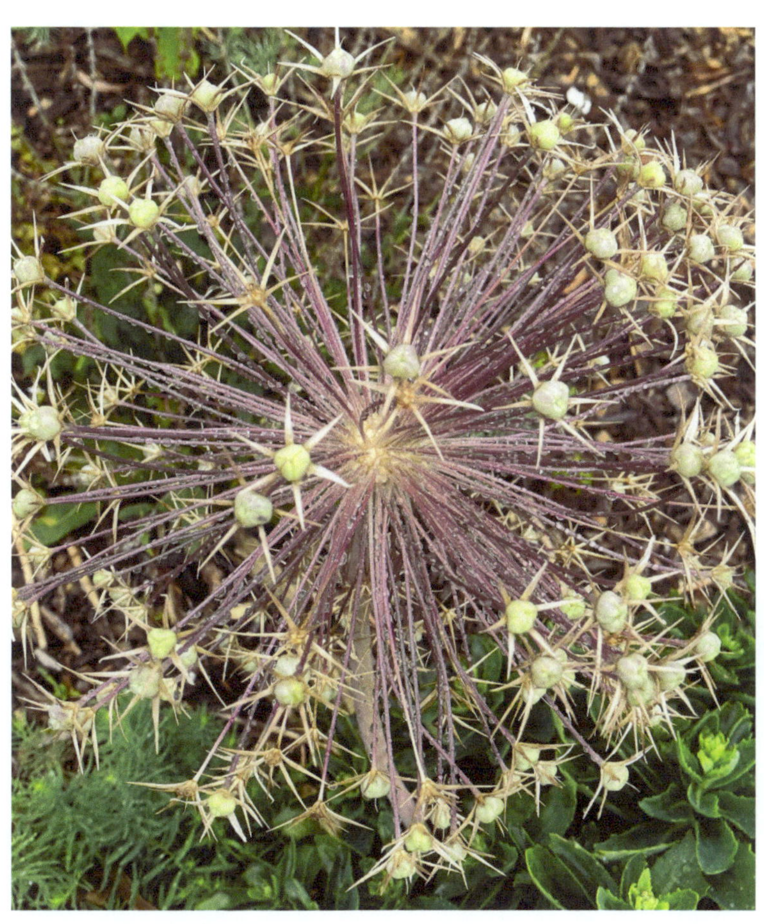

Thirst

It's only
By detaching
Your bucket
From the
Empty well
That you'll find
Satiation.

Smoke and Mirrors

Those who stand
In judgment
Of your reluctance
To continue fighting
An engulfed home
With a garden hose
Are what's honestly
In need of being
Extinguished.

Speechless

It's not about finding
The perfect thing
To say
It's about being perfectly fine
With saying
Nothing.

Conservation of Energy

Gate valves
Protect physical resources
By controlling output
Adeptly installed boundaries
Serve to preserve
Emotional well-being.

Dress Up

The human vessel
Of the soul
Holds identical enchantment
As an empty gift box
To a child.
Exploration of inner treasure
Dismissed
In favor
Of complacency
With surface value.

Rapt

Showing curiosity
About others
Through thoughtful questions
Is a gift
Yielding higher returns
Than one capable
Of being returned.

Heartsease

A beautiful life
Is marked
By the recognition
Of ordinary abundance
Versus the pursuit
Of enticing encumbrances.

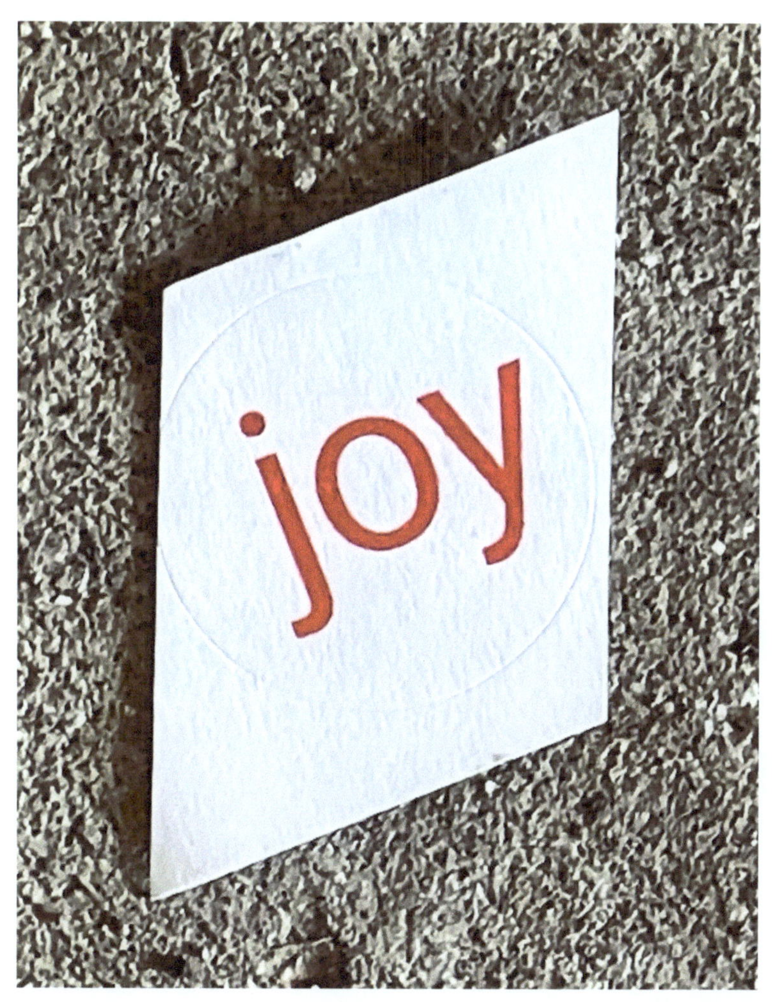
joy

All In

Vulnerability
Is a fork
In the road.
Decide
Whether to lean
Into the open heart
Or flee from essence
Of self.

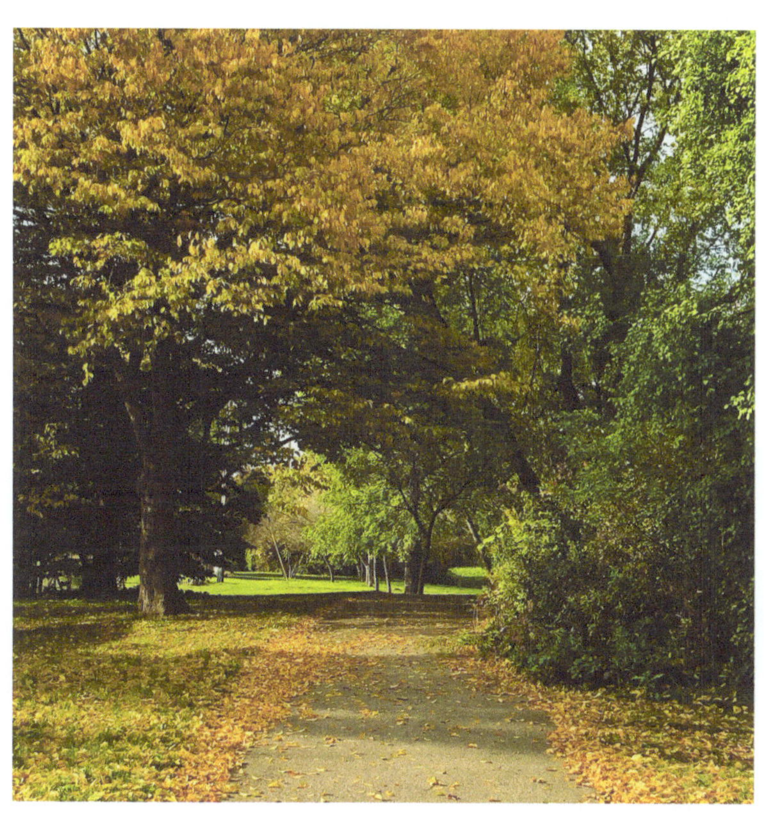

Preparing to Merge

What is
Doesn't present
With a green light.
Flashing yellow arrows
Denote the route
Of reentry.

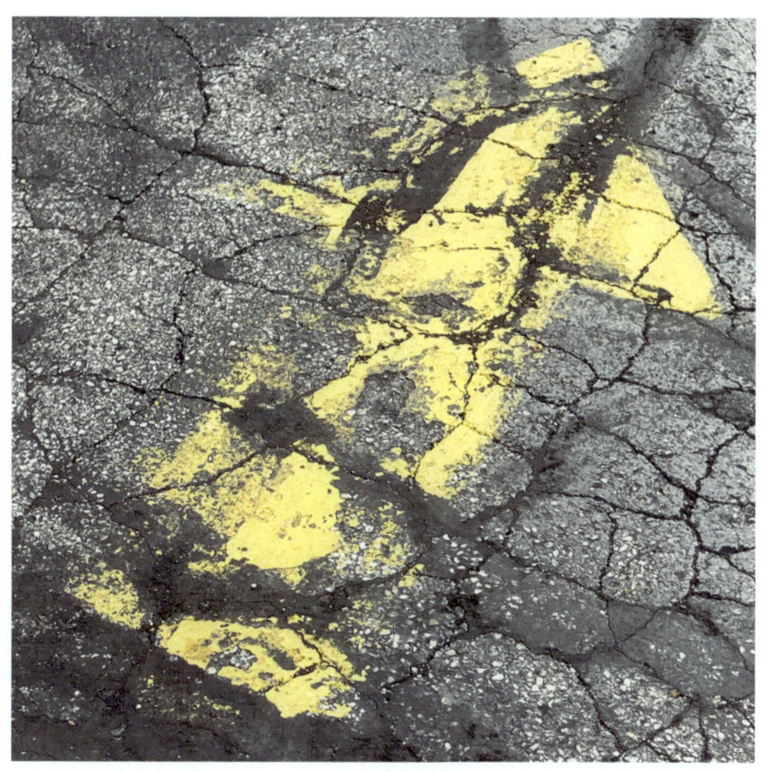

Sequel

Creating a new story
With a character
From another's tale
Requires a plot
That's stranger than fiction.

Checkmate

When embarking
On the game of life
With a token
That's not your own
Achieving victory
Isn't in the cards.

Raw

Returning to the stove
In an attempt
To cauterize
An old burn
With a new one
Is a recipe
For despair.

Roundabout

Unlimited rides
On the
Same carousel
Are no better
Than one
Because perspective
Remains unchanged.

True Gift

The wrapping paper
Becomes abraded
In transit
But the contents
Of the package
Retain their value.

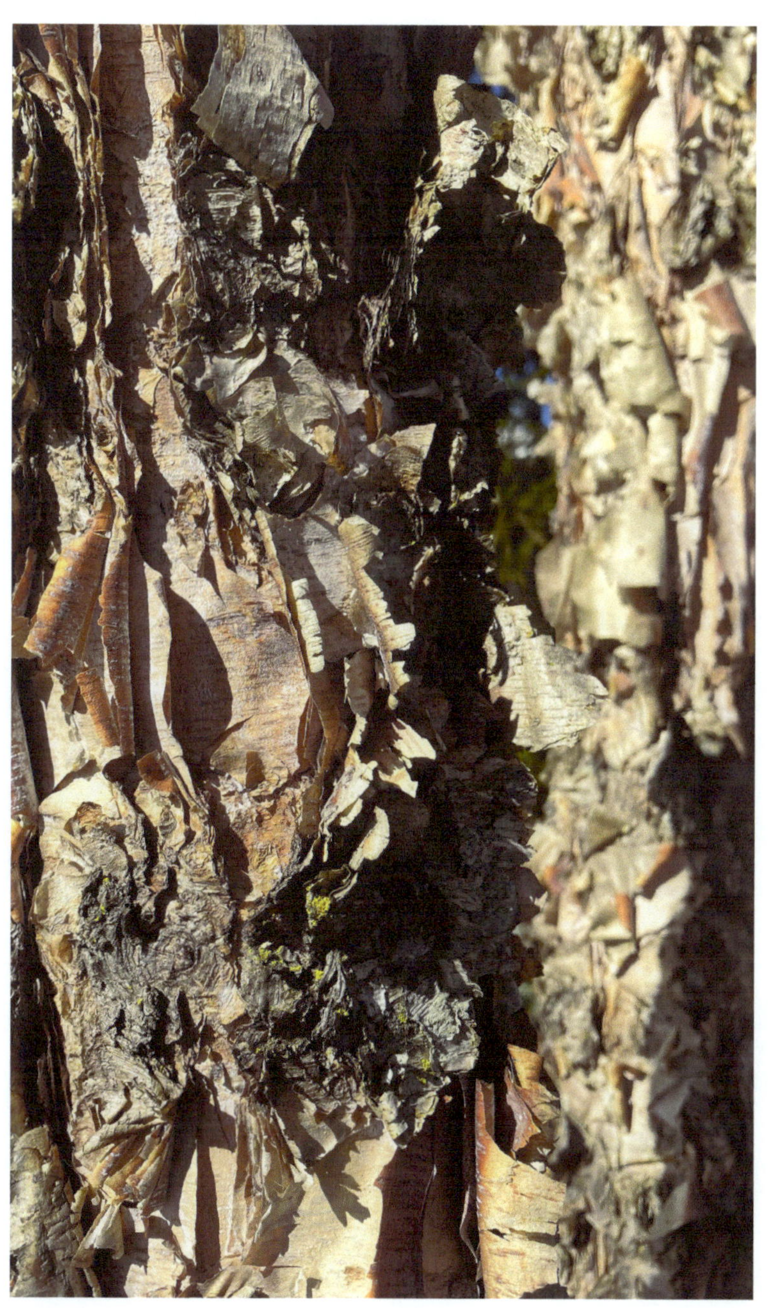

Not-So-Empty Cradle

Whereas midlife
Renders earthly bodies
Barren
Creativity and hope
Come alive
In heart and mind.

Flipped Switch

The fertile body
Prides itself
On sustaining others.
The elder body
Delights in
Nurturing authentic self.

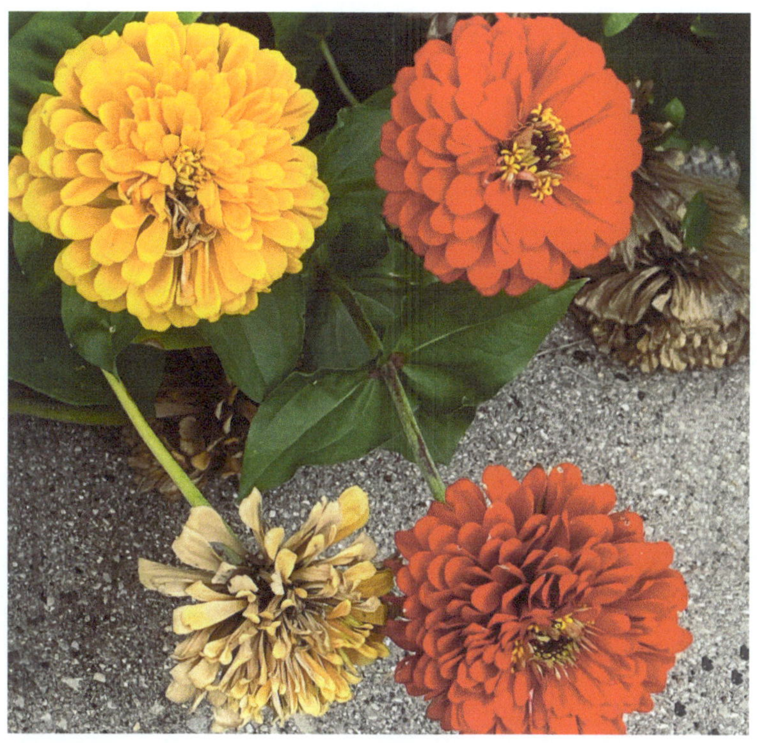

Third Act

In this stage
Like a storied
Evergreen tree
Roots remain
Tethered to earth
Whilst highest self
Surrenders to sky.

Get a Grip

A mug's handle
Provides a barrier
Allowing safer contact
With something innocuous
That could
Bring pain.
The same
Can be said
About our intuition.

Leaving Port

When the time comes
To untether mooring lines
The duration of dockage
Will have served
To make my hand
Steady enough
To captain the rudder.

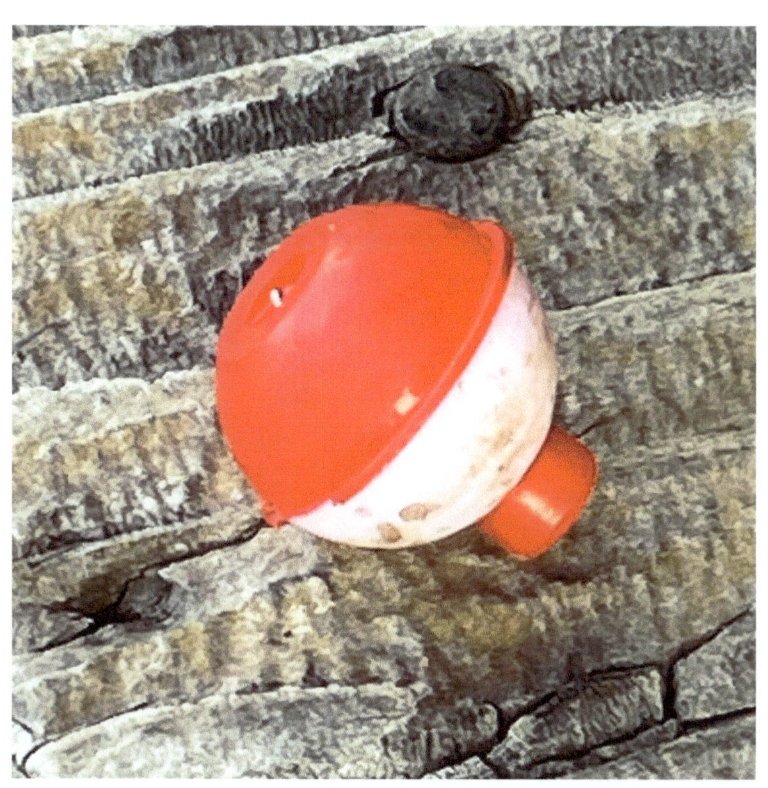

Modern Fairytale

There's no such thing
As Superman
Knights on white horses
Don't exist
Being your own
Fiercest protector
Is how the story ends.

Showtime

The curtain
Will inevitably
Fall.
Focus instead
On the quality
Of the performance.

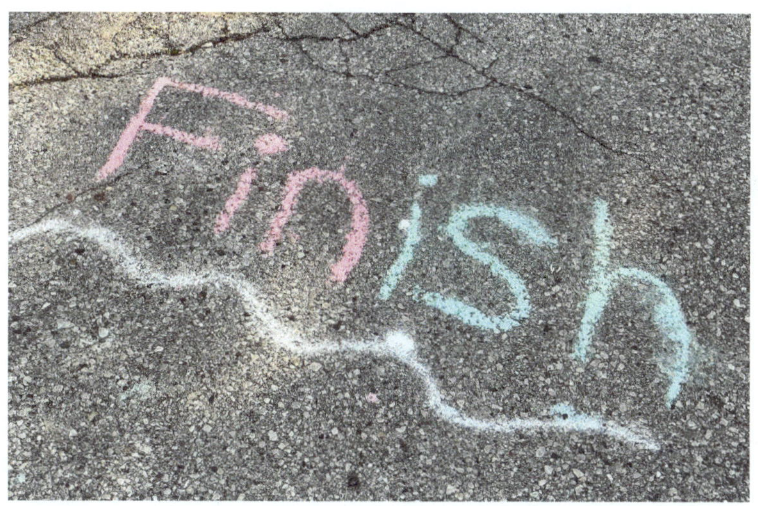

Nature as Sensei

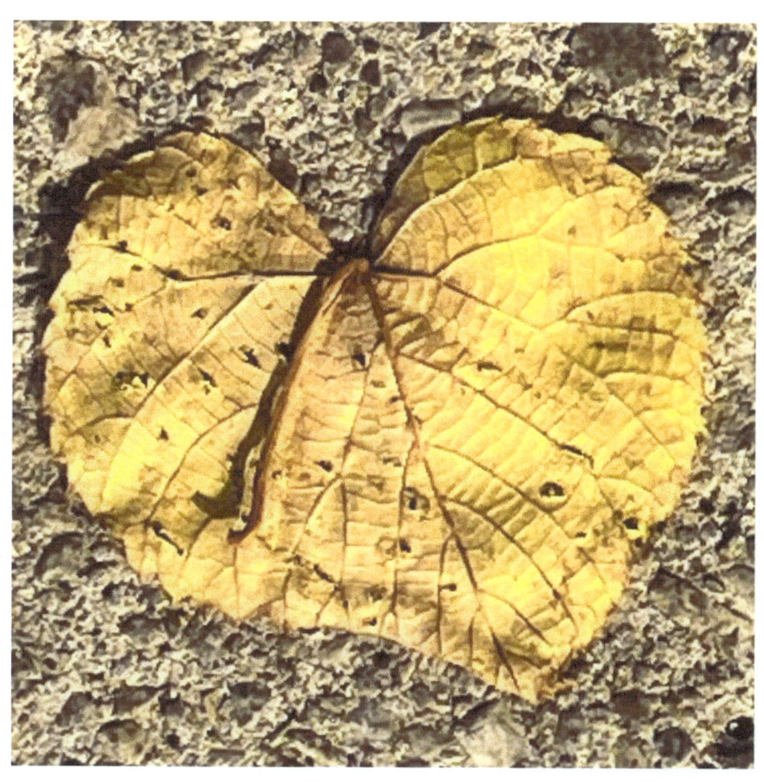

Grounded

It's not
Preventing exposure
To the existence
Of darkness
That makes flowers
Reach for the light
It's their choice.

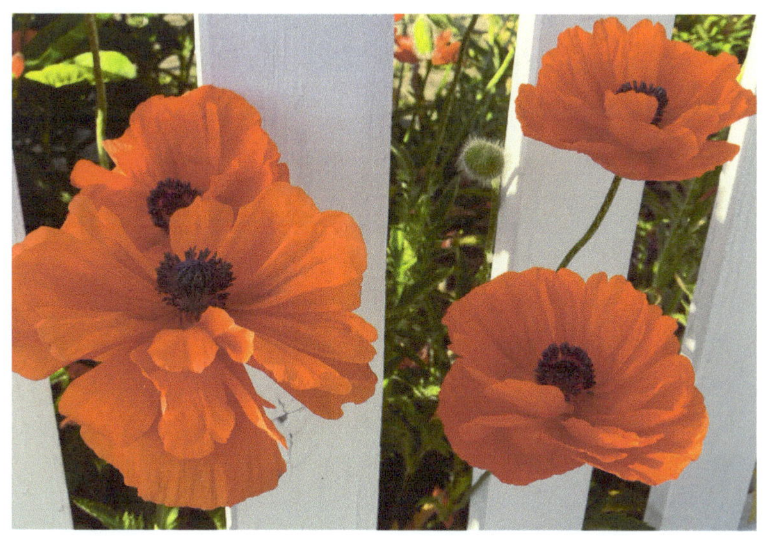

Flower Amidst Weeds

The same soil
That nourishes the graceful tulip
Sustains the wispy weed.
The eye of the beholder
Assigns value
To one
Over the other.

Diversity

Coral and golden-hued roses
Thrive side-by-side
On the same bush.
When will we recognize
The beauty of differences
Enriching the experience
Of our humanity?

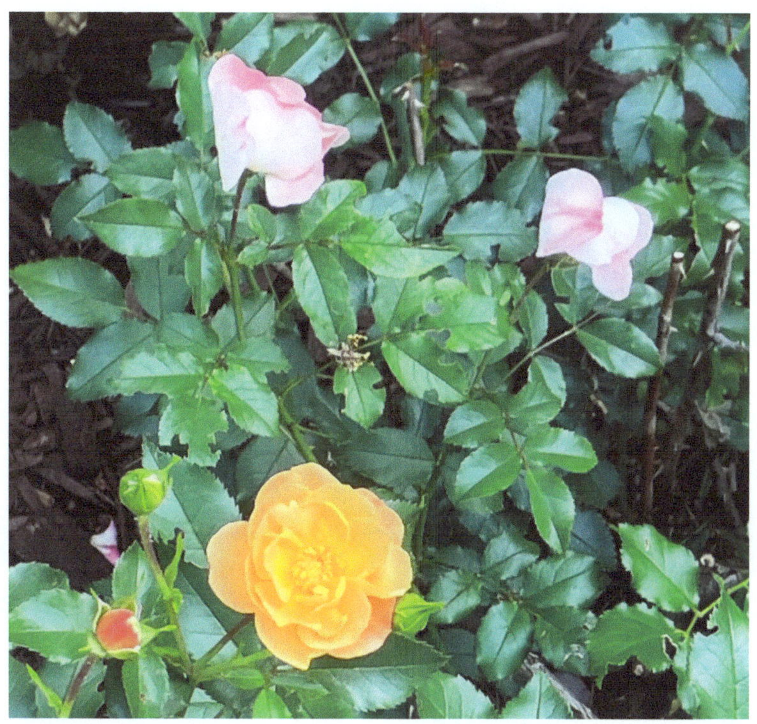

Armor

Not unlike
Rough bark
Concealing
The life story
Of a tree
Defense mechanisms
Protect
Brutal truths
Of the heart.

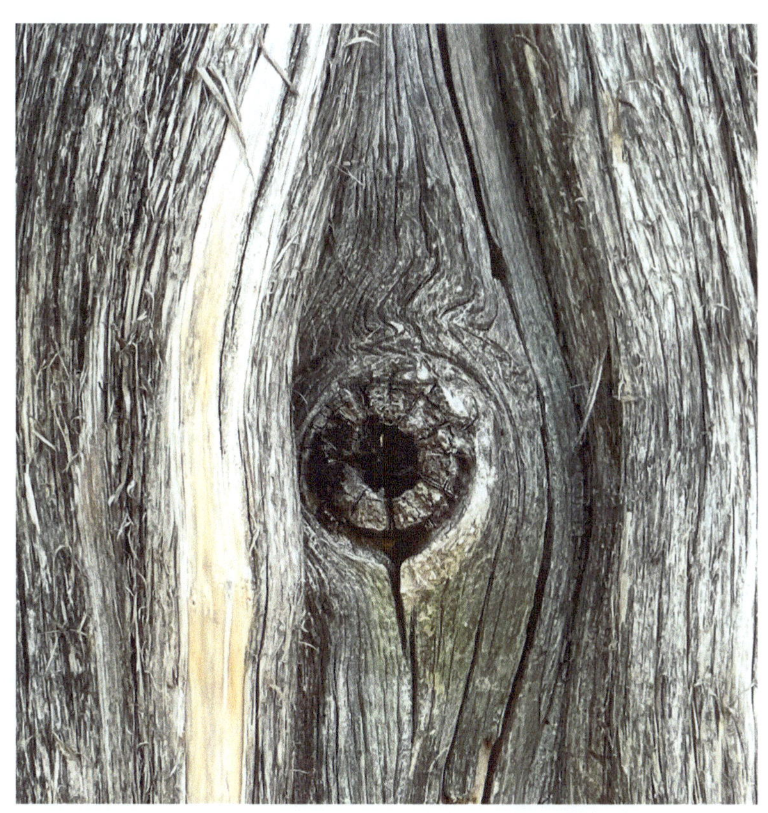

Internal Alarm

Whilst earthly anxieties
Withhold sweet slumber
Spotting the elegant moon
Soothes my soul.

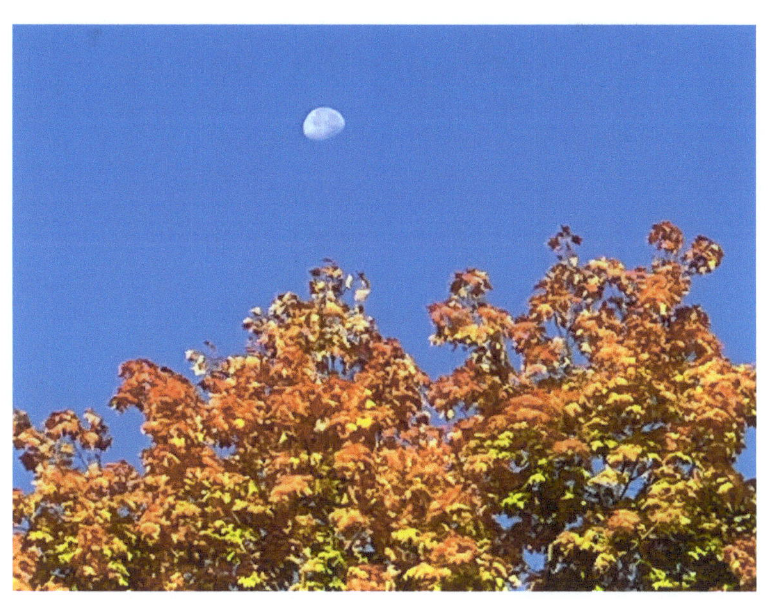

Hothouse Flower

When outer world conditions
Serve to stymie optimal growth
The nurturing cocoon
Of separation and serenity
Allows her burgeoning blossom
To emerge into the world.

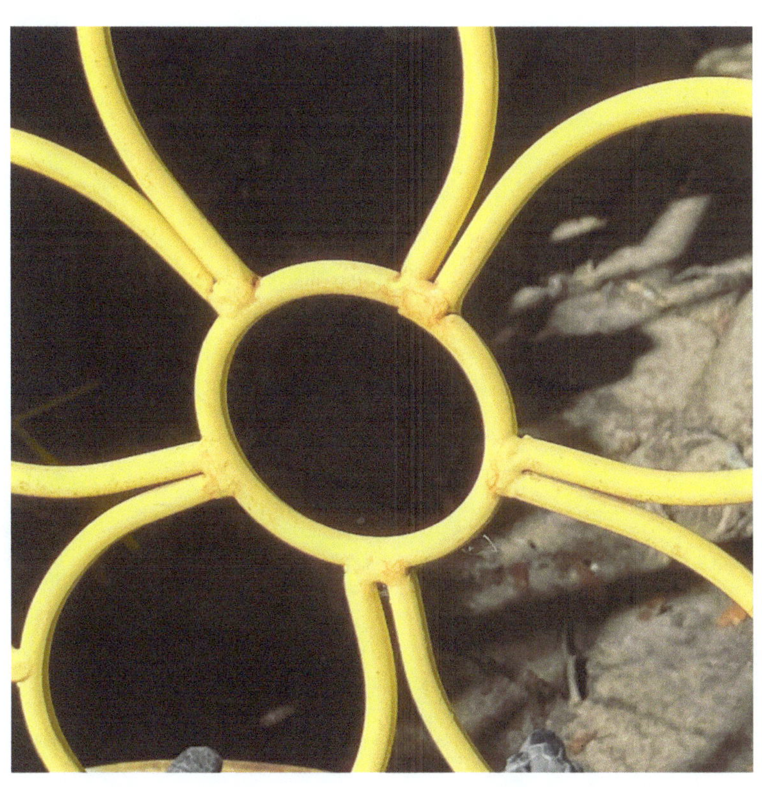

Spent

The stately sunflower
Hangs her head
Not in shame
But in repose
From well-shared abundance.

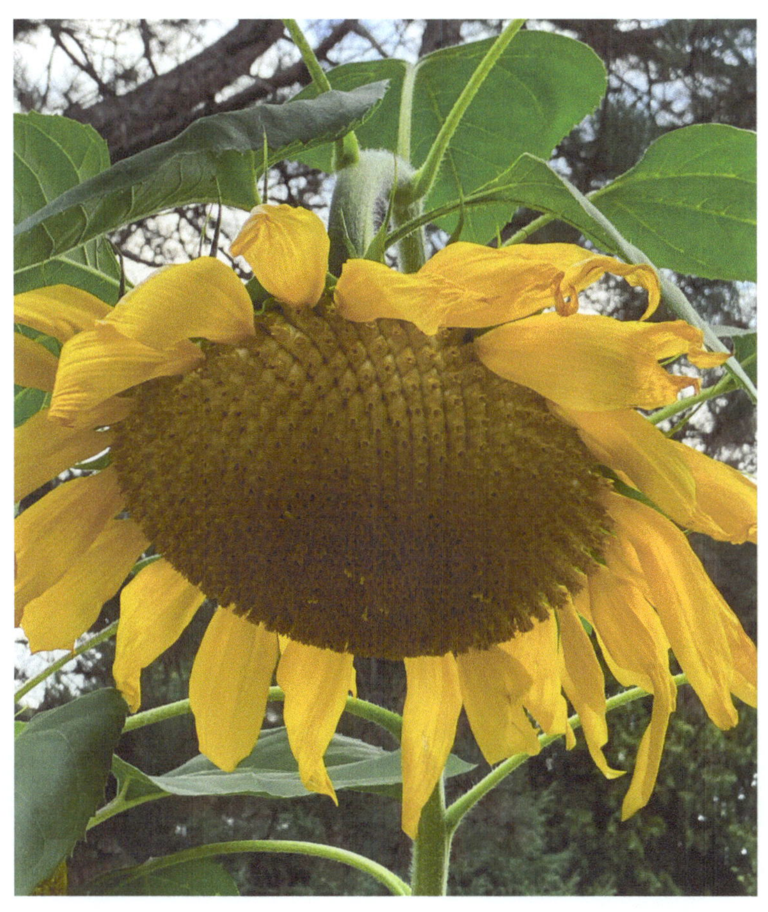

Deeper

Even when
The outer magnetism
Of the flower
Is exhausted
Its inner beauty
Brings about
Its continuance.

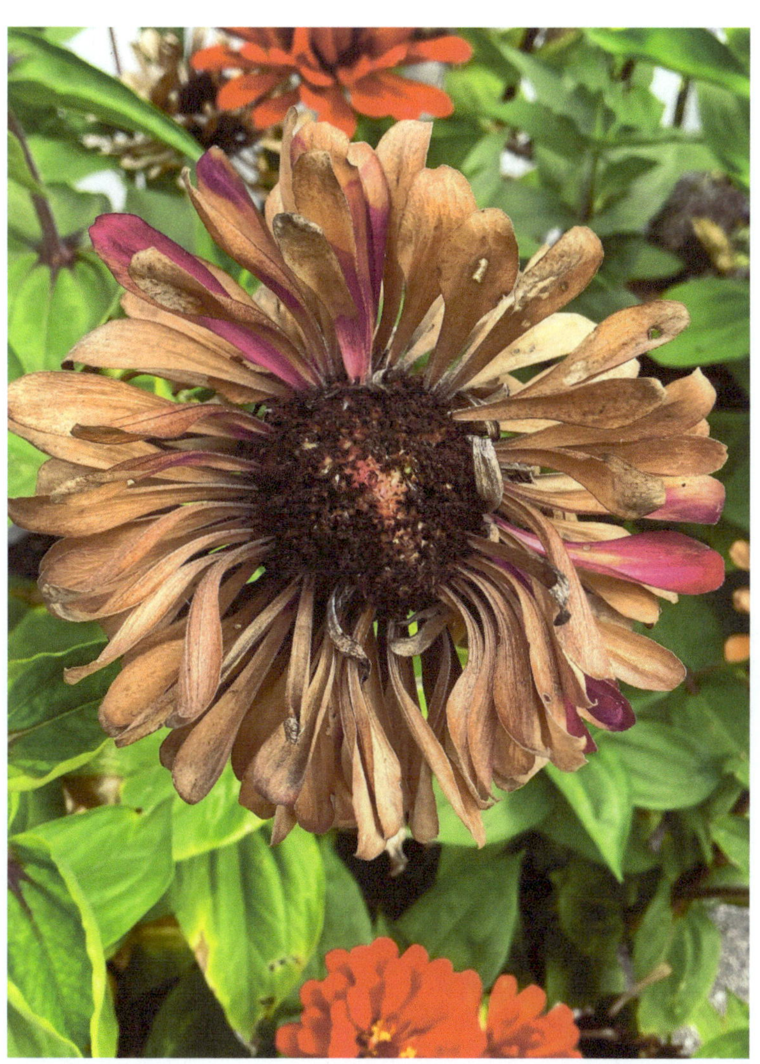

Deadheading

The act
Of pruning
What's expired
Is necessary
For plants
And people
To achieve
Optimal growth.

Moxie

The badass flower
Stands its ground
Daring to bloom
In the middle
Of harm's way.

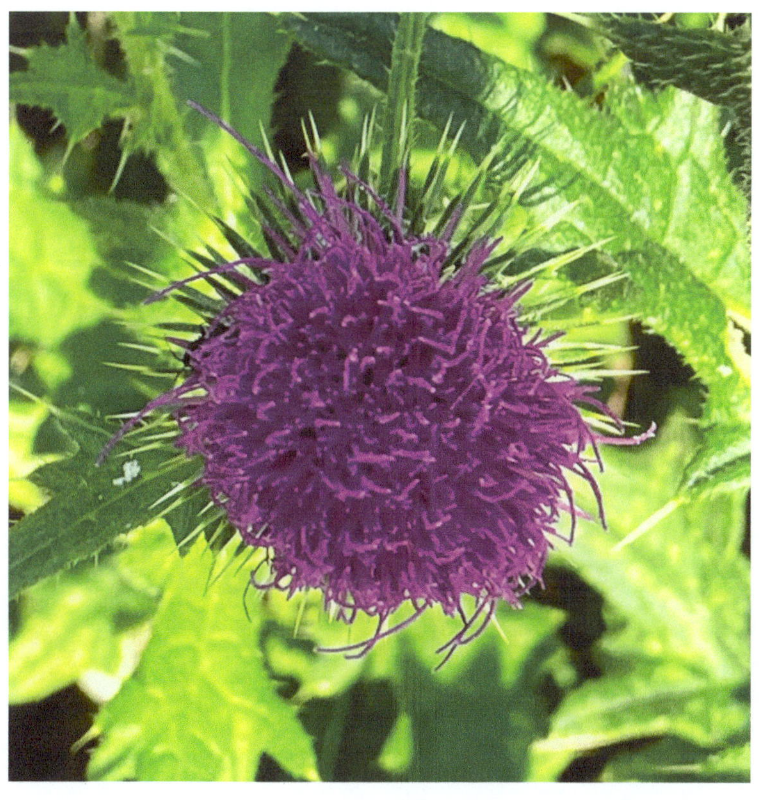

Flourish

The exuberance
Of the ethereal peony
Transcends the containment
Of its terrestrial stem.
Be a peony.

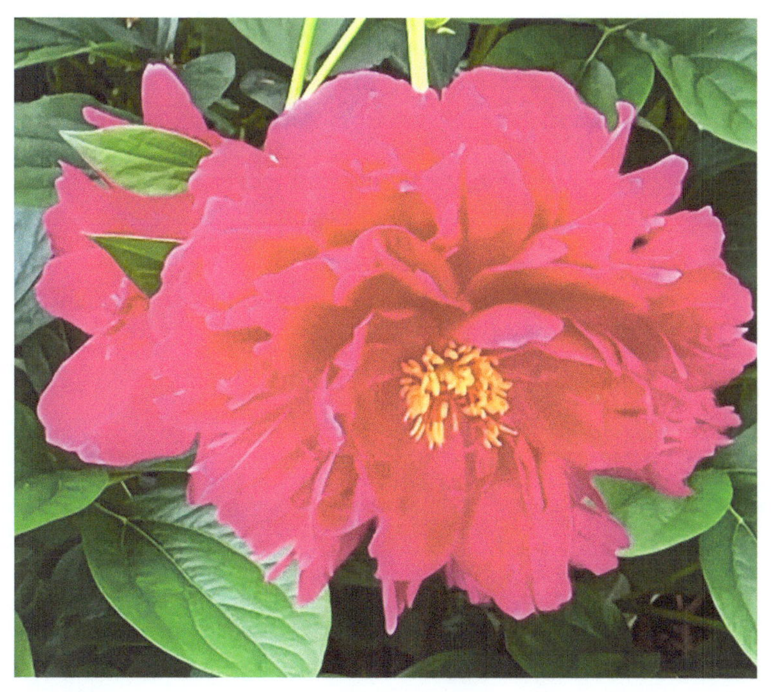

Moving On

When the time comes
To end its tenancy
With a tree
The autumn leaf
Confidently lets go
Drifting dreamily
To Mother Earth.

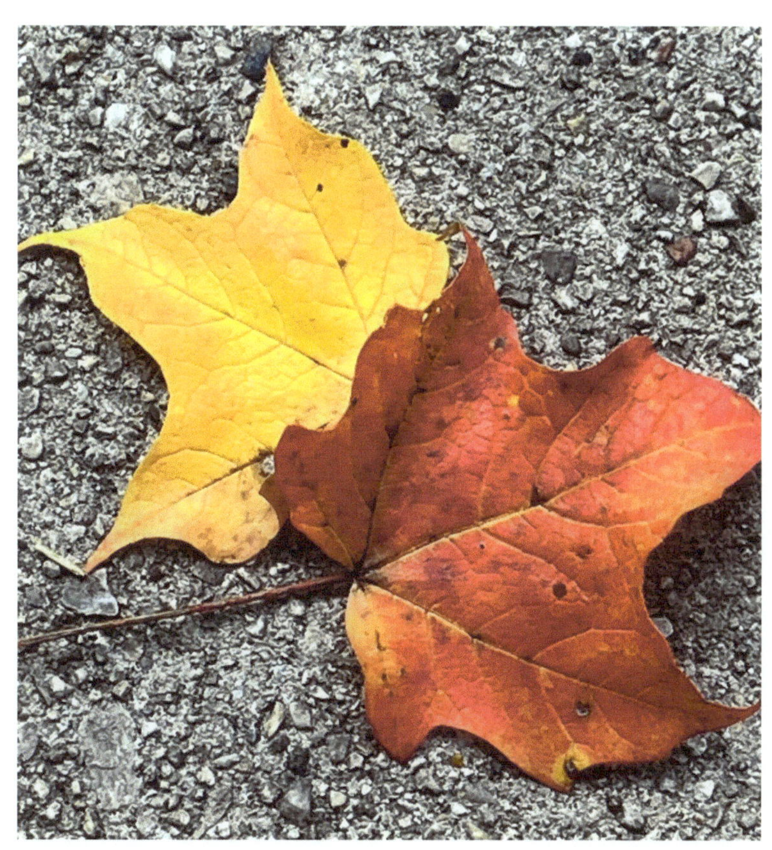

Coupling

The falling snow
Perfectly molds herself
To the form
Of the branch
Contentedly aware
This graceful spooning
Has a season.

Enlightenment

As the rising sun
Gradually transitions
The western sky
Through various hues of blue
Nature reminds us
Profound change
Is often initiated by
An imperceptible process.

Enoughness

An advanced soul
Is gratified by
Merely observing beauty.
An unseasoned soul
Suffers unrelenting desire
To possess it.

Flow

Just like leaves
Dancing to the beat
Of unseen fall breezes
Our pneumas
Can be similarly moved
By assurance
In the divine.

Groundbreaking

When embarking
On a new path
Without debris
Remember the unstable footing
Of the previous trail
Provided fortitude needed
To appreciate
Being unencumbered.

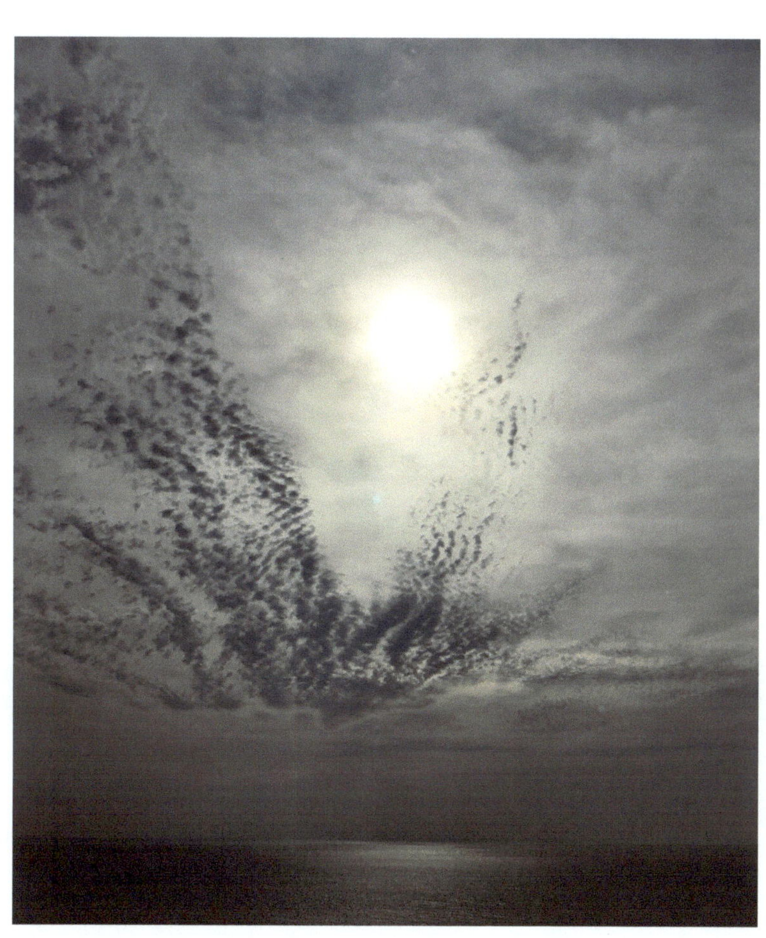

Ensemble Cast

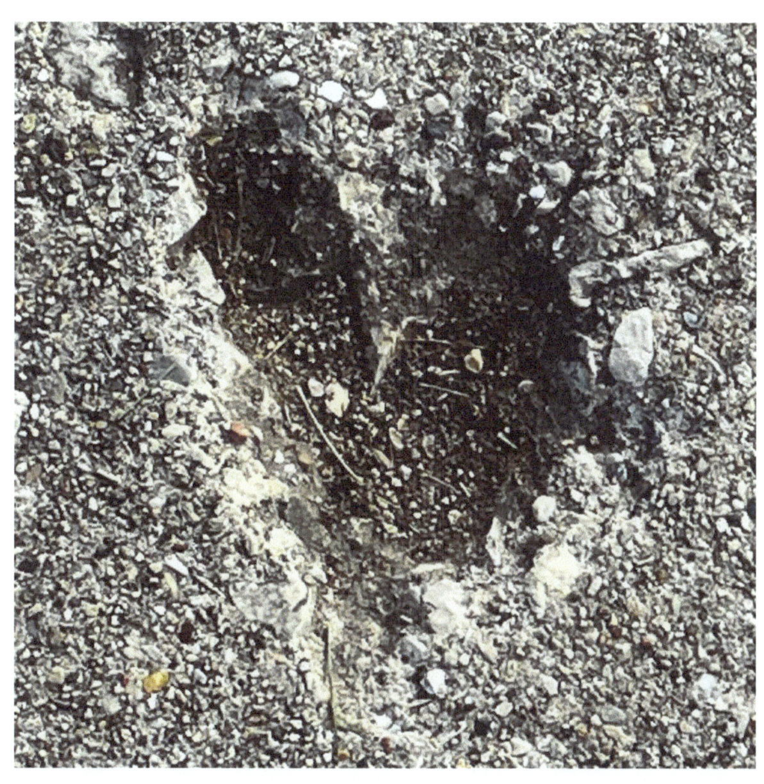

Never-Ending Story

During earthly tenure
We live together
Live together apart
Live apart together
It's only when
Our celestial souls
Depart terrestrial confines
The purpose of
Interconnection is revealed.

Lone Rider

You arrived
On a motorcycle
Covered in tattoos
Unapologetically genuine
From the outside in.
When you returned order
To what was disjointed
Contentment was restored
To my heart and mind.

Unmasked

As you sat
Across from me
Deep in conversation
Not only
Did you see me
You truly saw me.

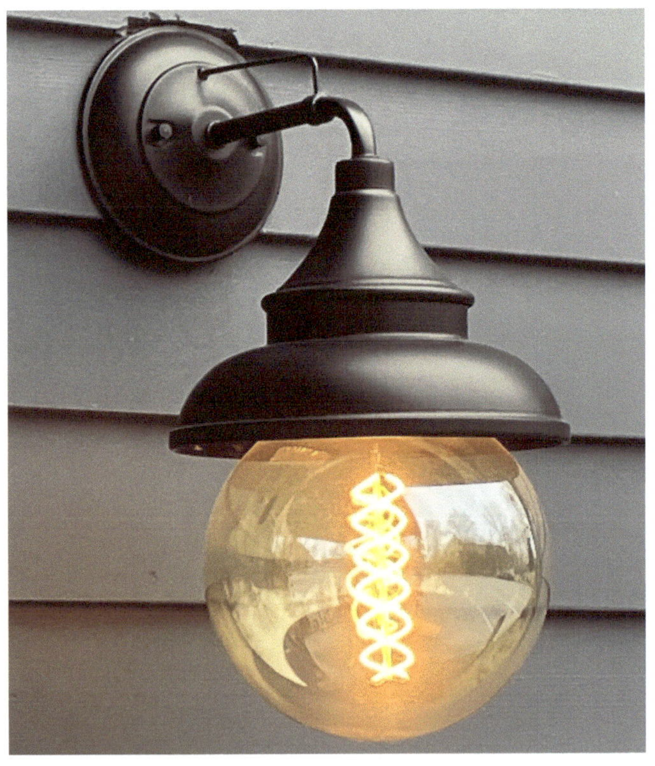

Beautiful Unknown

After we
Held hands
After we
Locked eyes
The grandfather
Clock tolled
And your
Spirit passed
Through me
As it
Passed on.

My Circus

Failing to boldly face
Elephants in the room
Changes what should be
Carefree and fortifying
Into a shitshow.

Full Disclosure

Because I exist
On the periphery
Of your life
Being privy to
The complete story
Is achingly impossible.

Quiet Storm

Be wary
Of the seemingly
Docile scorpion.
Feigned passivity
Doesn't lessen
The pain
Of its sting.

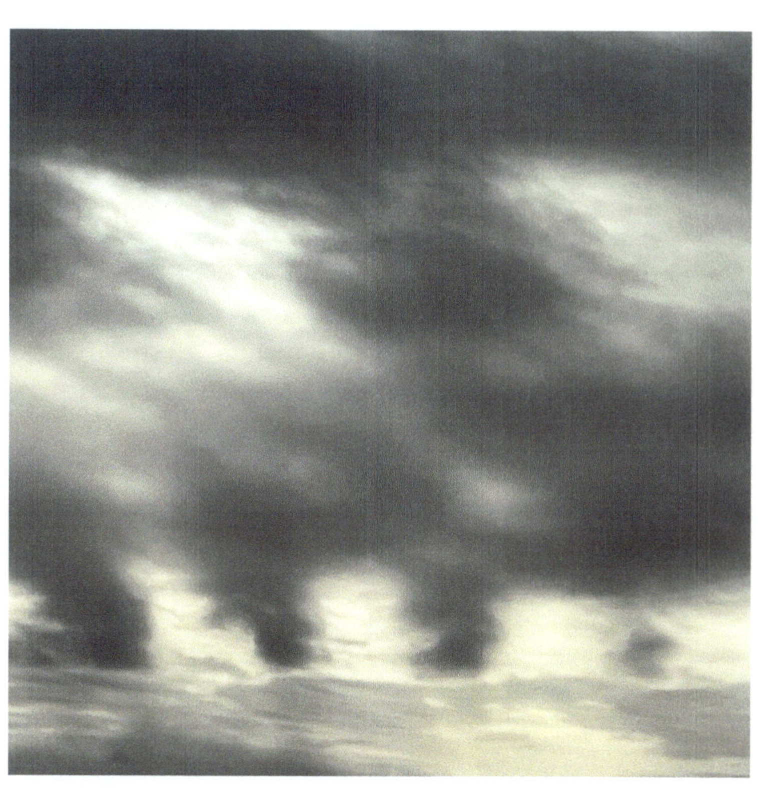

Flame Thrower

You
May be impervious
To the heat
Of the fire
But
My retardancy
To the flames
Has expired.

Twofer

We used to be
A package deal
Two for the price of one.
With that promotion
Now expired
Responsibility for marketing
The desirability of your contents
Lies with you.

Well Done

It takes two
Fully cooked individuals
To create
A new recipe
For interacting.
The transformed side
Of the pancake
Cannot be flipped
And returned
To its raw state.

Changeover

When the time comes
To pass the baton
Whether it's dropped
Defiantly or carelessly
My heat
Of the race
Is complete.

Drawbridge

Choosing to remain distant
Isn’t
About despising
You.
It’s about
The necessity
Of caring from afar
To accept
You
As you are.

Autonomy

When you choose
To let go
Of the handlebars
And cease running
Alongside the bike
It actually liberates
You both.

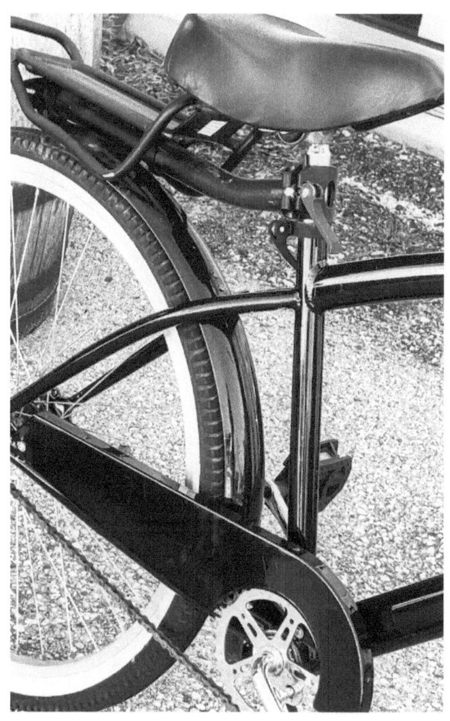

Apple and Tree

Your terrestrial body
Grew inside mine
Your celestial spirit
Was already complete.
I planted virtues
Living in strict
Accordance with them
Your heart served
As a sieve
Filtering them to
Match your truth.
You needed my body
To belong
To this earth
But you never
Belonged to me.

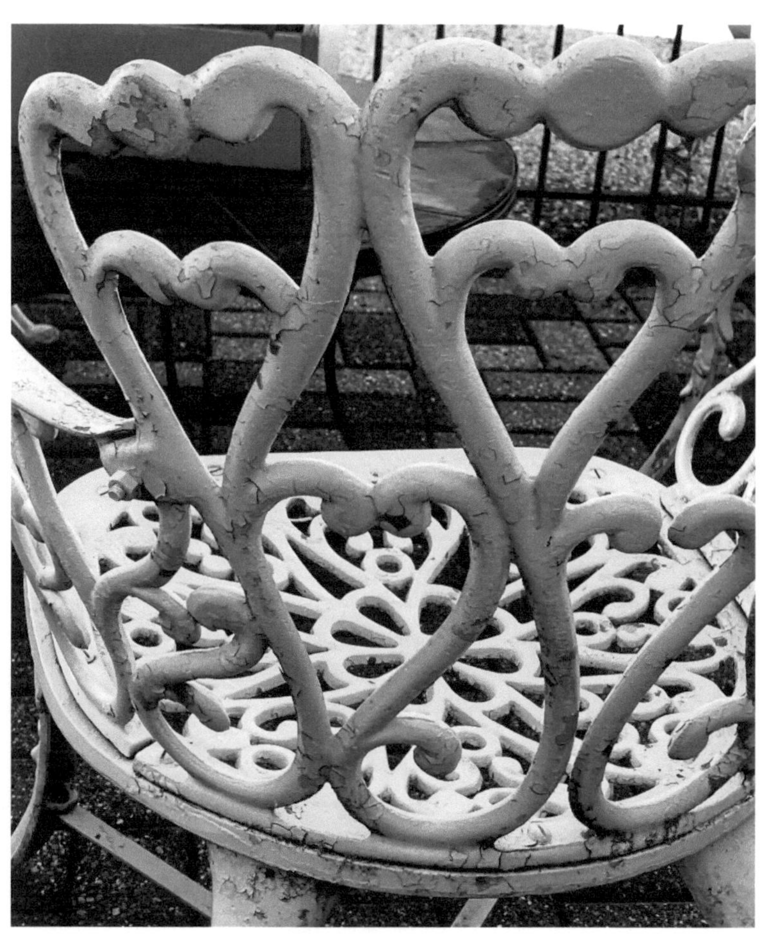

Matters of the Awakened Heart

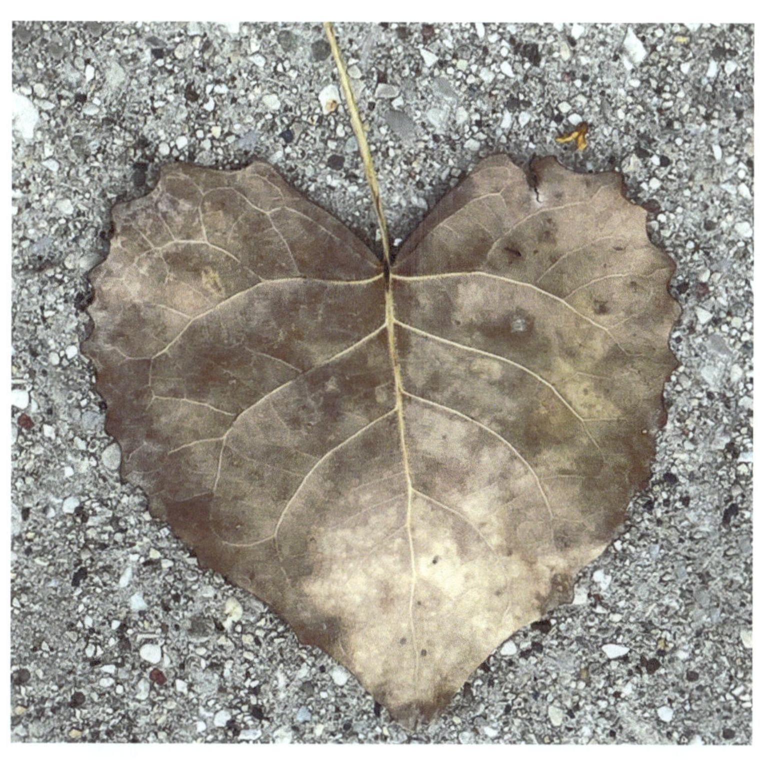

Mixed Signals

Just because
Two people
Come together
In time
And space
Doesn't guarantee
Their hearts
Being on
Similar pages.

Moving the Chains

Your contentment
With keeping things
Unchanged
No longer aligns
With my need for
Growth.

Joint Tenancy

If you're
Without a key
To your
Own heart
How could
You ever be
A steward
Of mine?

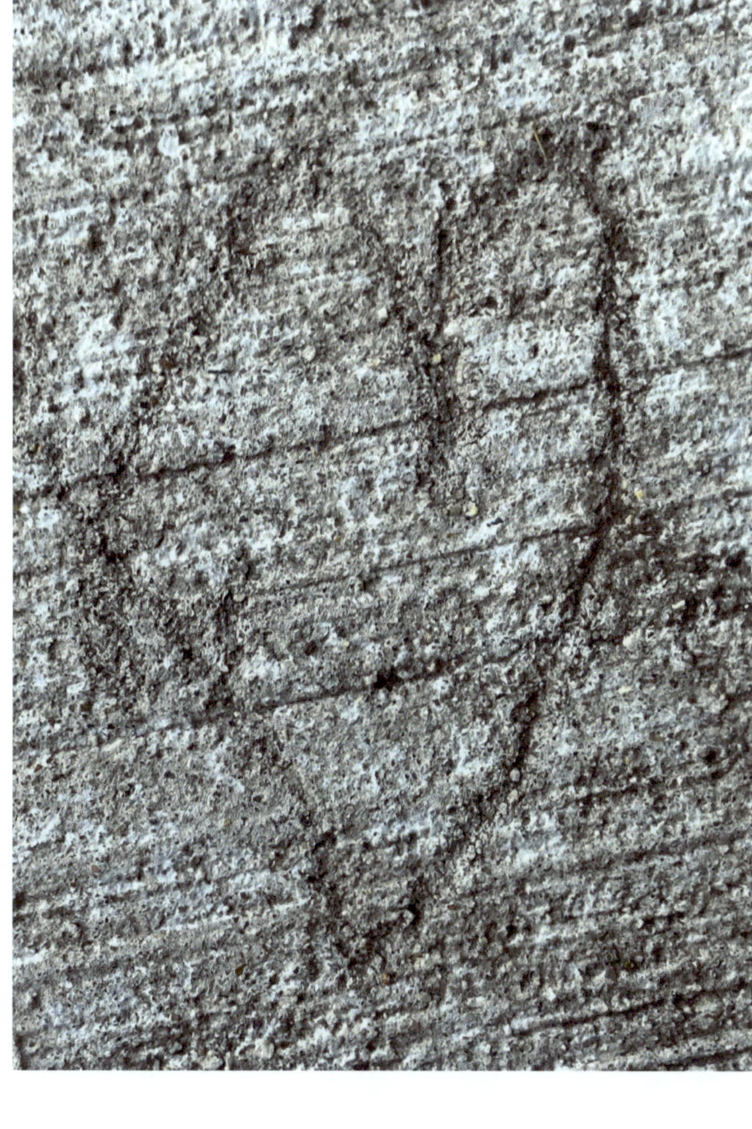

Eden

My ripe fruit
Is just out
Of your reach.
It'll require
An extension
Of your investment
For harvest.

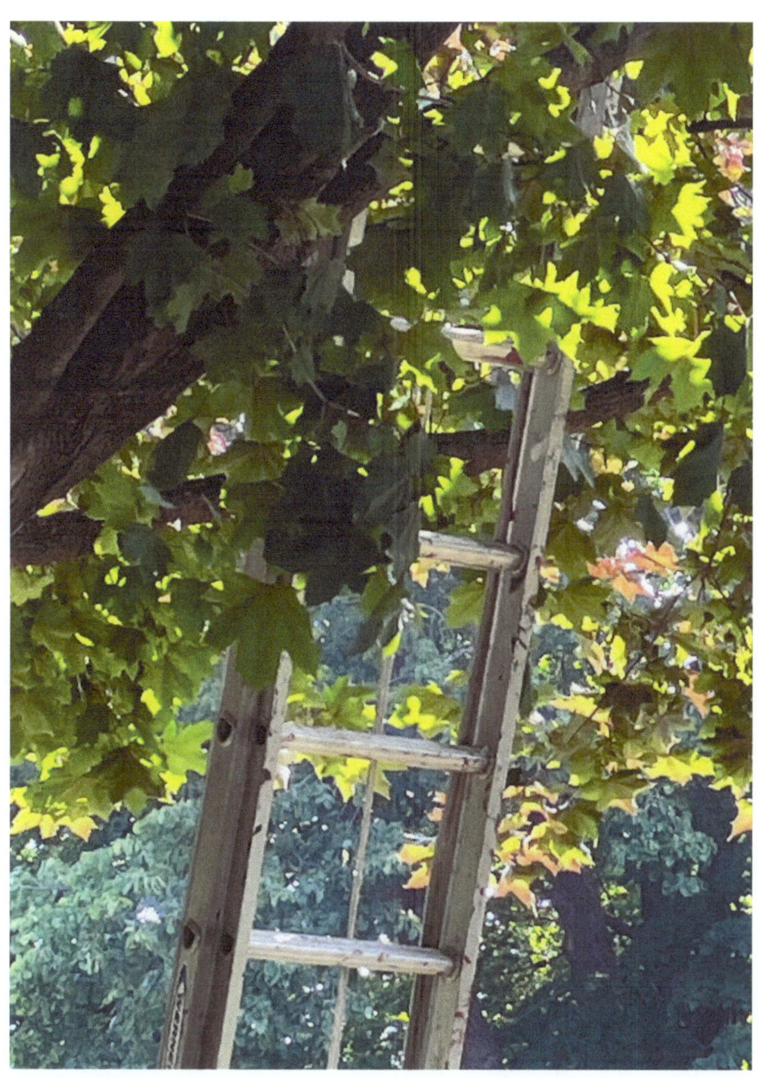

Pandora's Box

I fear
Tearing off
The festive paper
And sparkly bow
Will reveal
An absence
Of substance
In the package.

Heart RX

While my love
Has no expiration date
Automatic refills
Are terminable.

Heart Strings

I refuse
To make apologies
For the fact
My heart comes
With strings attached.

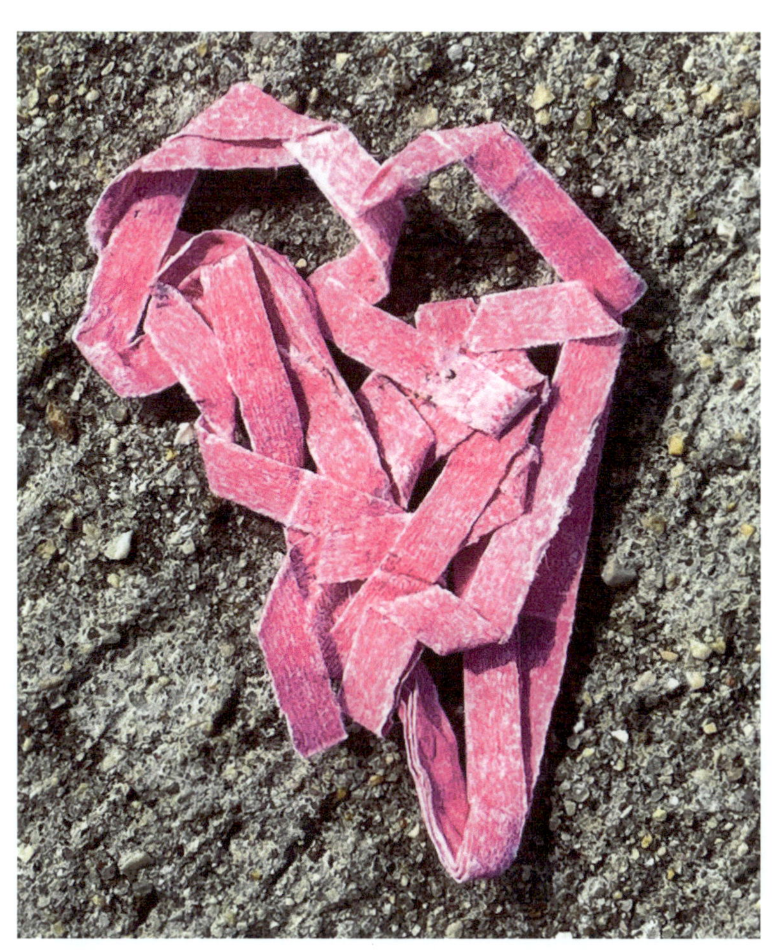

Undeliverable

I would have
Loved you
Through heartbreak.
Your indifference
To that gift
Serves to halt
Future care packages.

Slow Burn

You
Were an accelerant
Of smoldering ashes.
It's now time
For the responsibility
Of tending those
Flames to be
Mine.

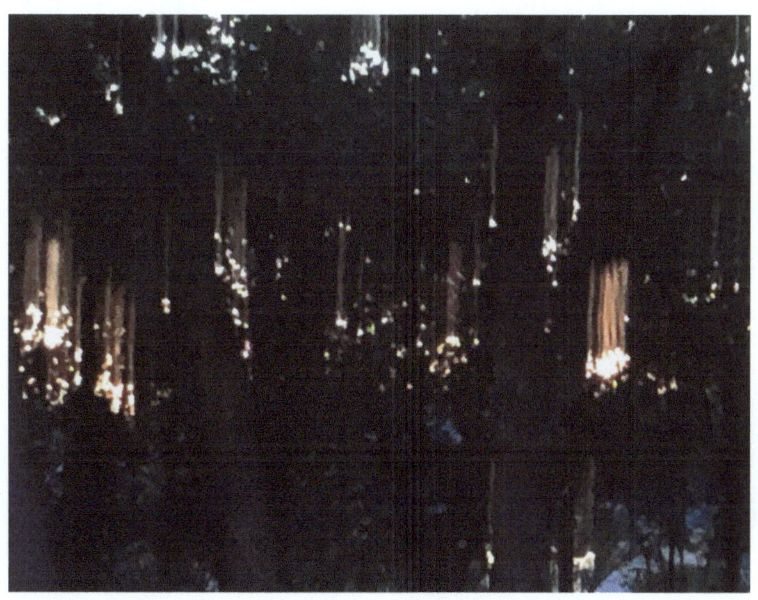

Seamanship

As my hands consummately
Navigate your longitude
Your trembling heart
Serves as the compass
Guiding me home.

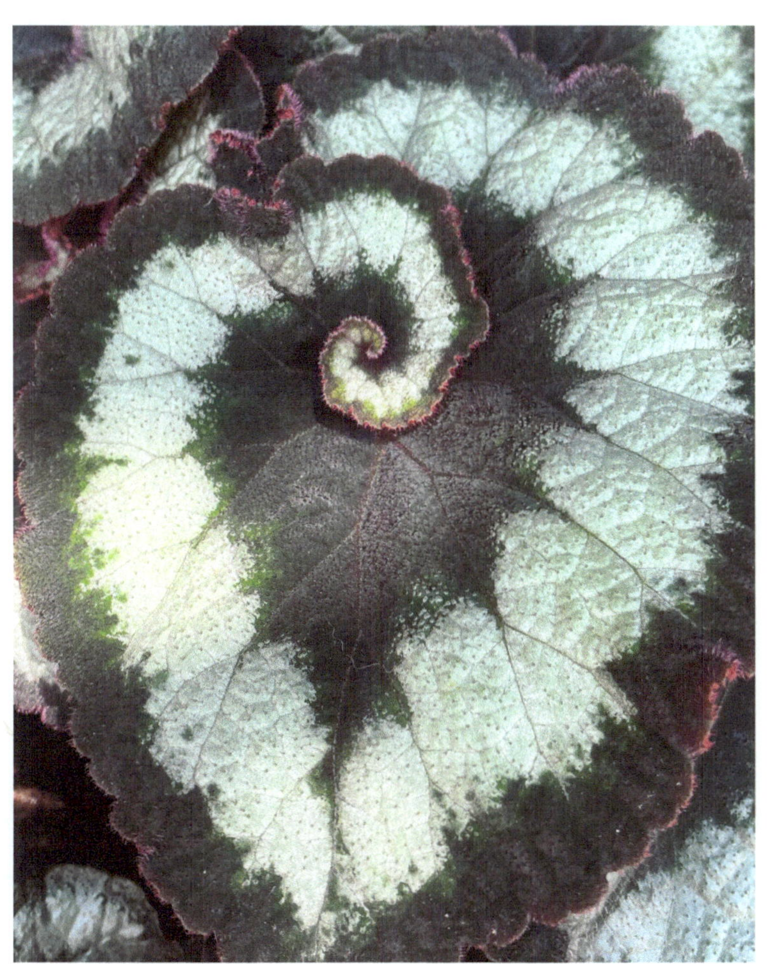

Fervor

If the heat
Of my mouth
Causes chocolate to surrender
Its solidity and melt
Just imagine
What I could do
To you.

Lights Out

Ensconce me between
Your arms and legs
Shield me from reality
Be my weighted blanket.

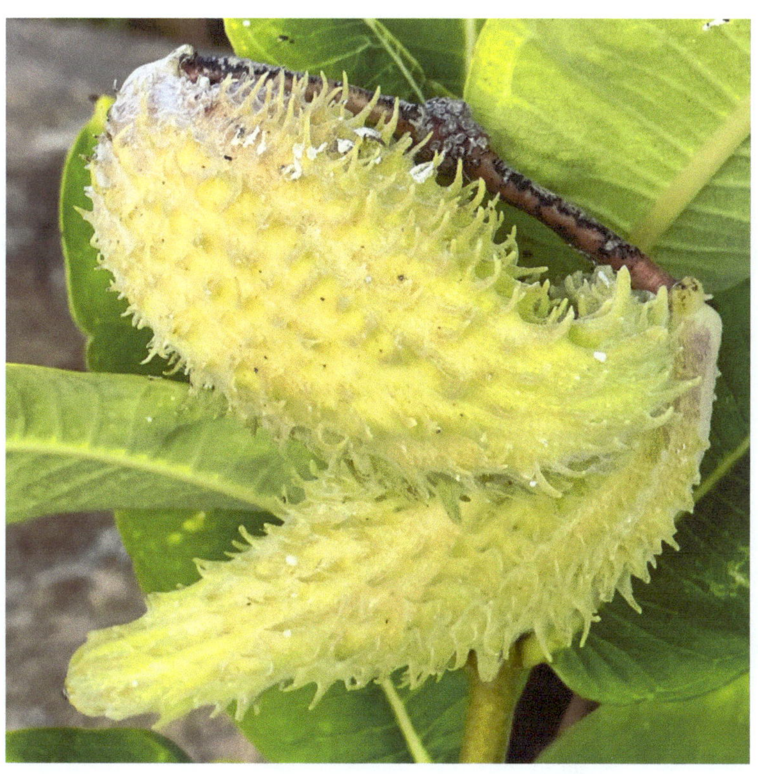

Real Deal

Truly loving someone
Means wishing
What brings
Wholeness for them
Sans thoughts
Of benefiting you.

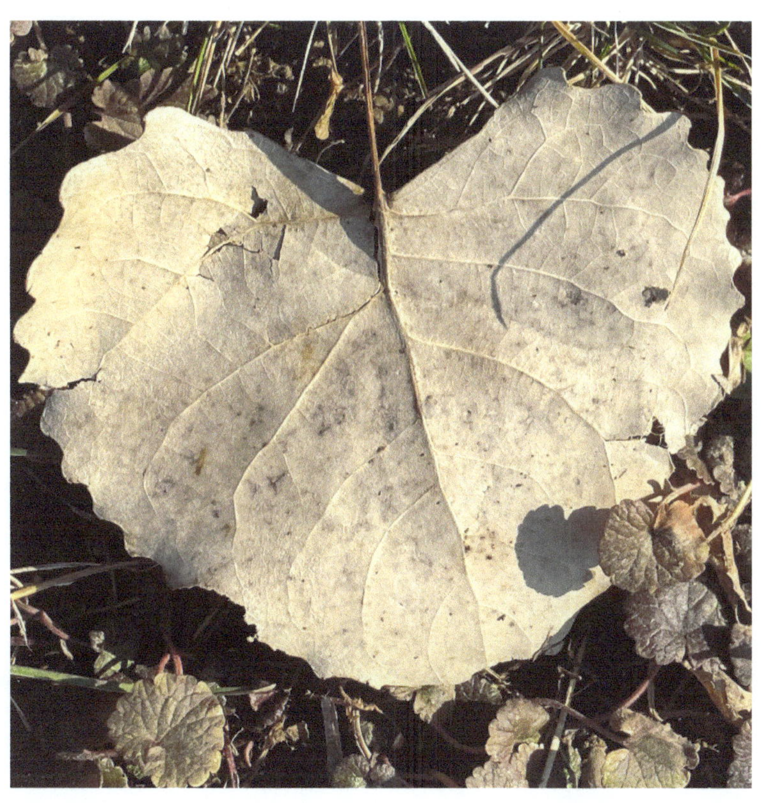

Just Friends

What a
Maligned motto
For another
Soul who
Cares for
Your heart.

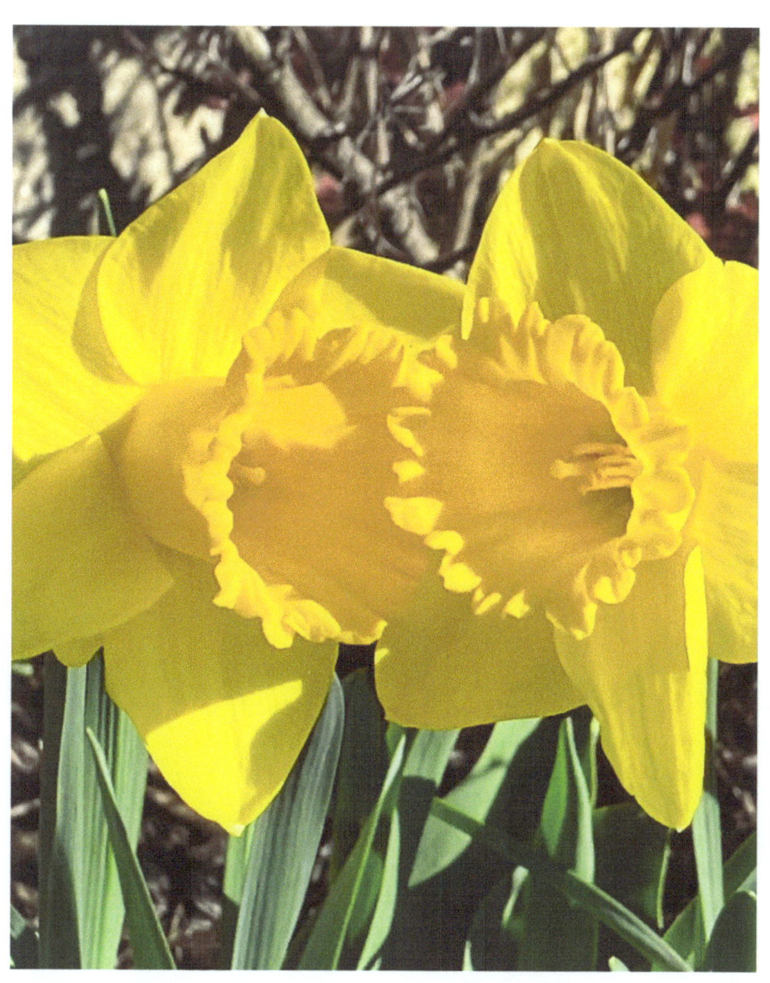

Misconception

With each
Silent day
Confirming separation
I'm left
With the realization
We were
Never together.
Ever.

In Flux

The hardest thing
Is when
Body and mind
Are ready
To move on
But heart
Still cannot
Let go.

Divergence

Relationships are like
A train station.
Although physically together
Souls hold tickets
For different destinations.

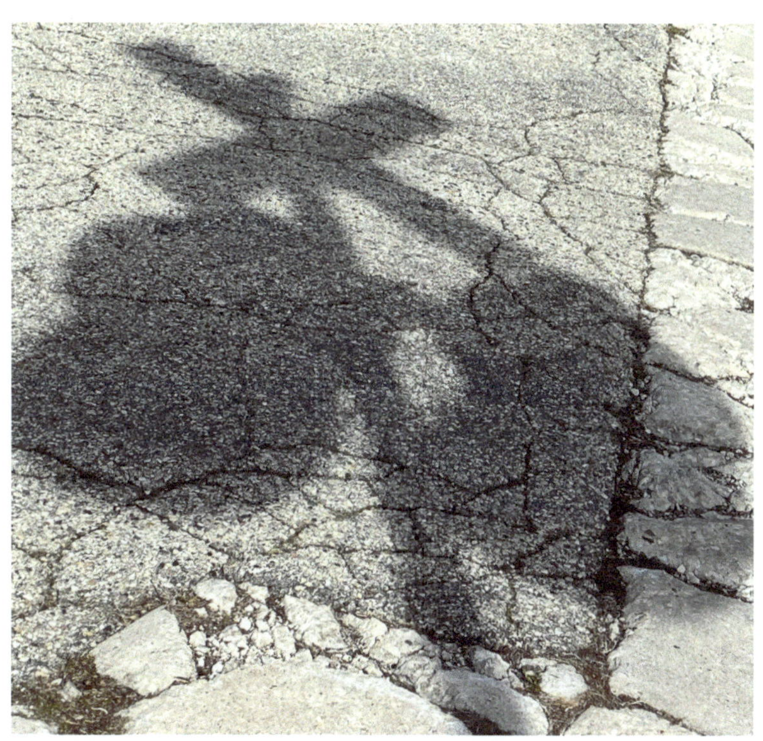

Heartbreaker

Choosing to love fiercely
While understanding the inevitability
Of reasons and seasons
Is a most valiant act.

Retitling

When you came
Into the picture
My untethered pieces
Lay scattered
At your feet.
Now I am
The glue
Holding the whole
Together.

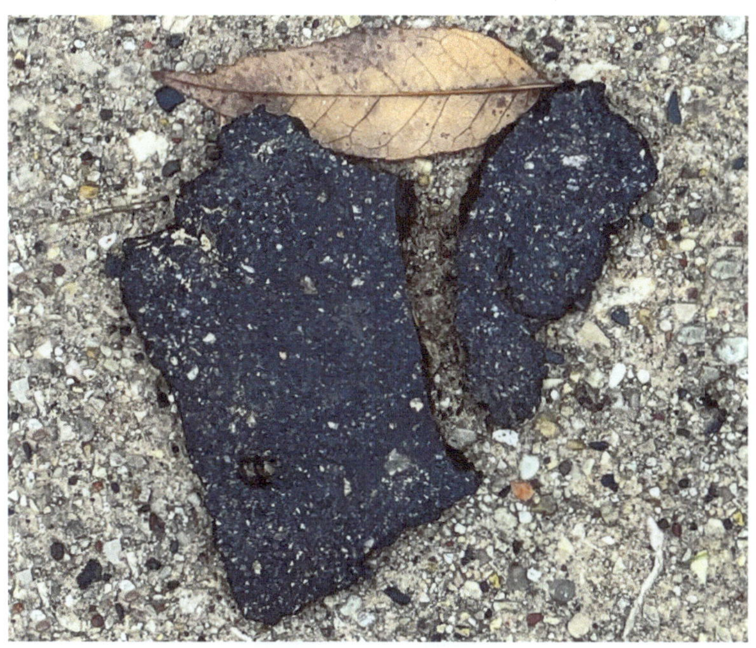

Self-Possession

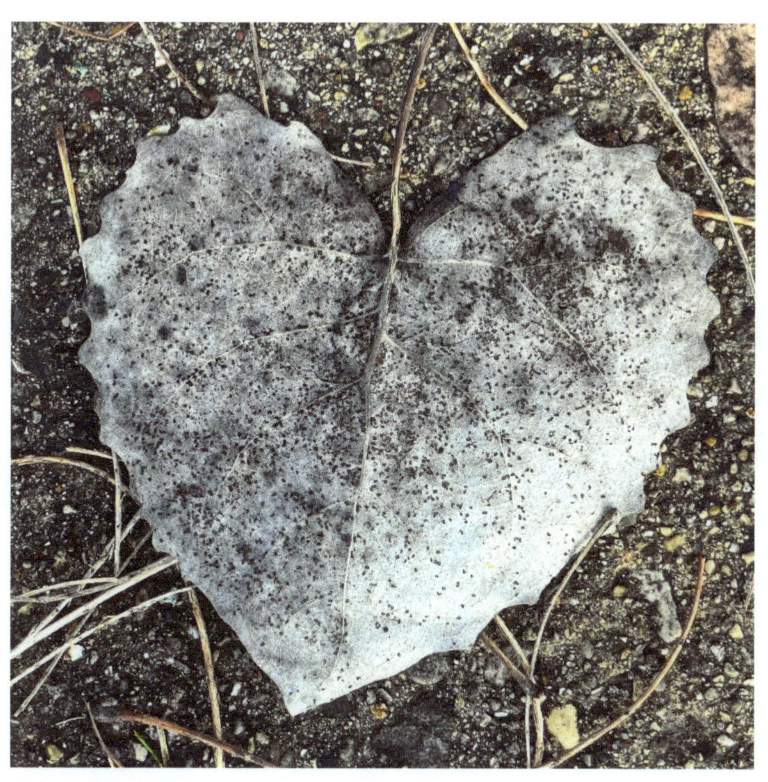

Cultivating Growth

My creative outlet
Used to be
Manicuring the grounds
Of my earthly abode.
Contentment now stems
In capturing prose
From the ethereal realm.

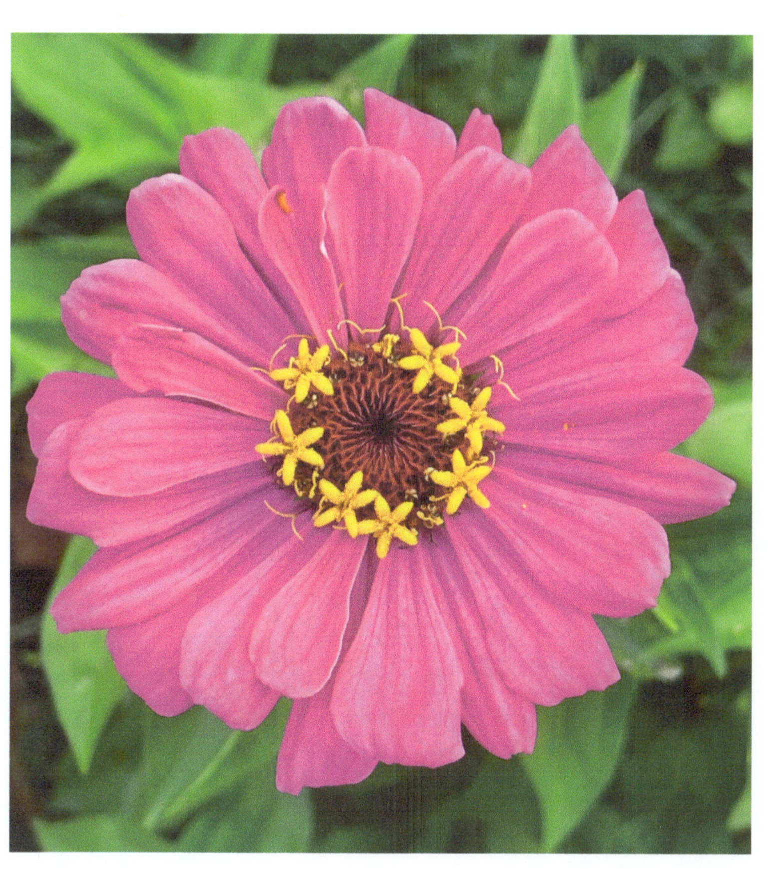

Downsizing

In life
Heavy decisions
Hinge on
Determining and jettisoning
Burdensome weight
In order
To soar.

Alteration

Humbly acknowledging
The costume
No longer fits
Allows for the hem
To be let out
Reinventing the garment.

Hesitancy

What's sadder than
Failing to change
Is completing the
Metamorphosis and refusing
To let go.

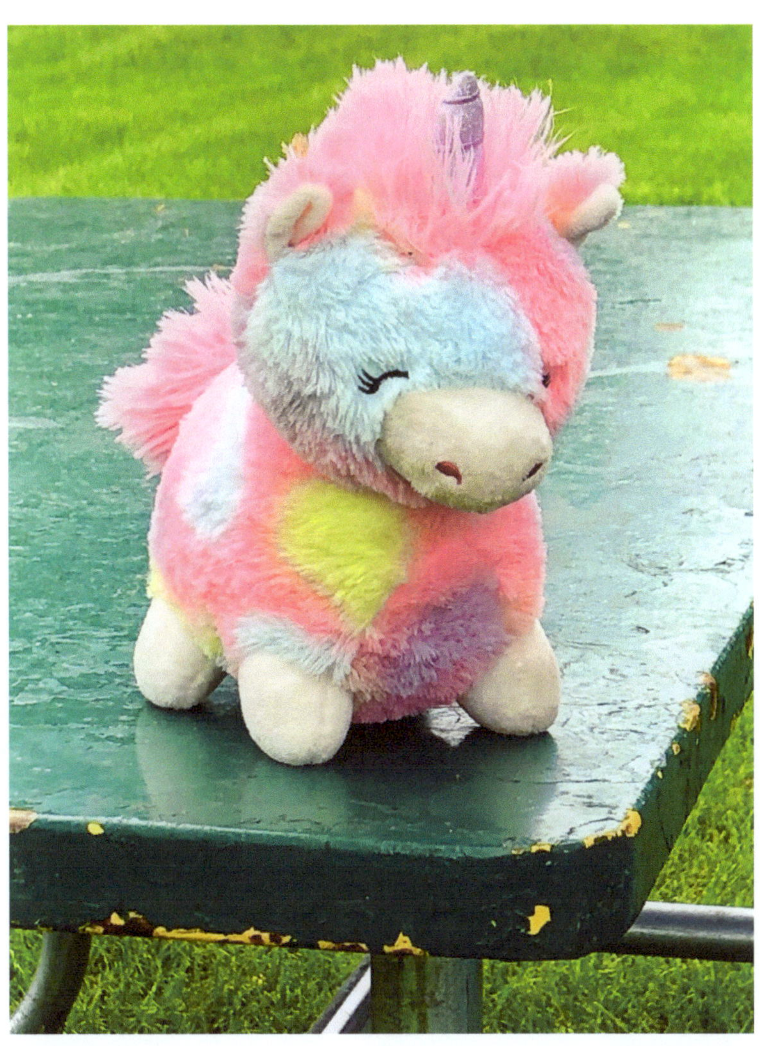

Silent Rebellion

That moment
When it's not
The 4th of July
And you wake up
Sprawled diagonally
Across the bed
And celebrate
Your independence.

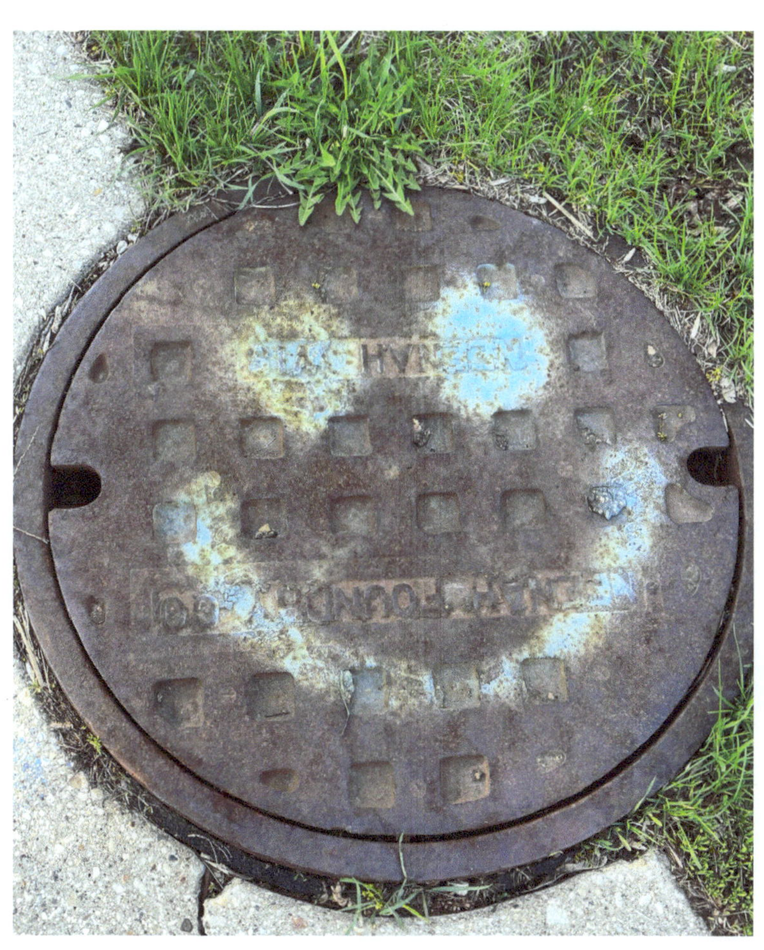

Calling the Shot

My needs
Used to go
Unspoken
For fear of losing
You.
My needs
Are now freely
Spoken
With confidence in finding
Me.

Partnership

This time around
My relationships
Will consist
Of two whole people
Uniting in peace
Versus two people
Coming together in pieces.

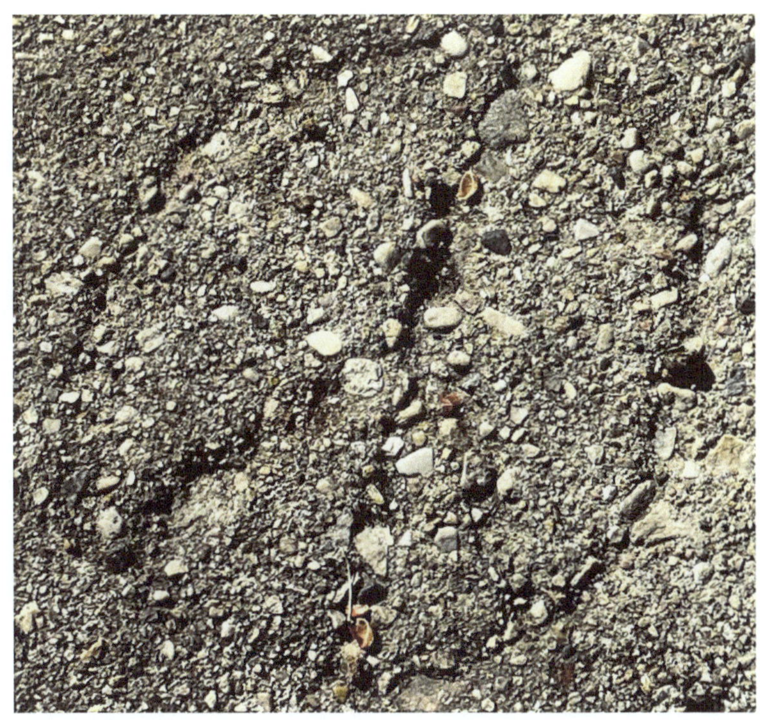

Long Leash

If you think about it
We are all rescues
Carrying wounds
From our pasts
Capable of being
Ameliorated through
Kindness and curiosity.

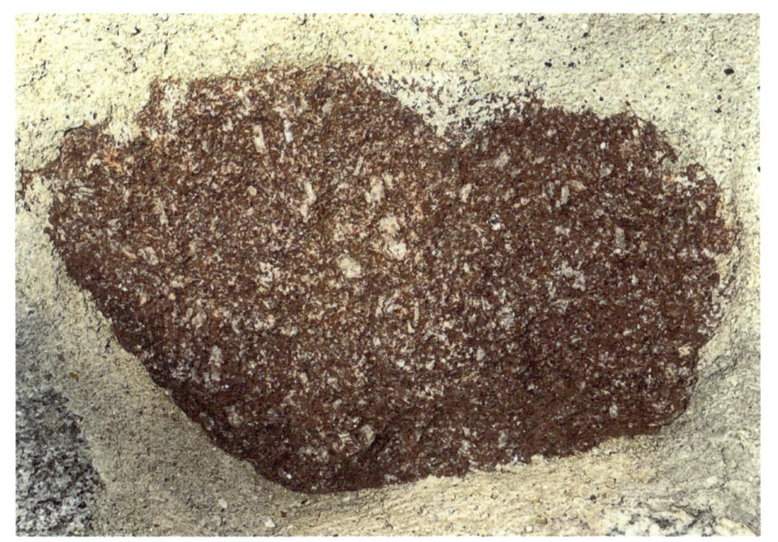

All-Inclusive

Life isn't
An opulent cruise.
It's a series
Of sandbars
Allowing for
Stillness reflection
and gratitude.

Countdown

Time please stop
I want to pause
Right here right now
I've just begun
Living authentically.
Earthly body's eyes
Newly awakened
To omnipresent beauty
Once fevered mind
Surrendered to stillness
Vulnerable heart
Abounding in tenderness
For self and others.

Rearview Mirror

When one chooses
To sit in
Awe and gratitude
It becomes clear
All the challenges
That took place
In the past
Served as framework
For the life
Enjoyed this day.

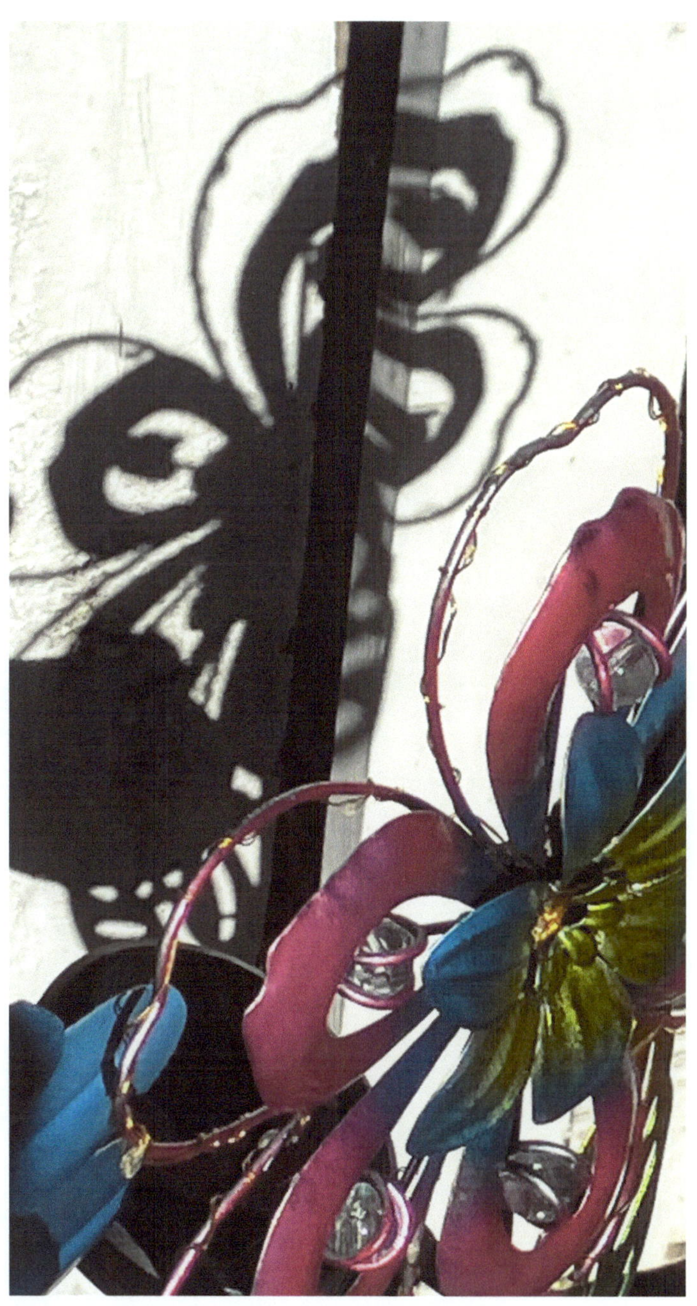

Turn of Events

How momentous
That the sanctuary
Of my body
Once ensconced you
From the world
And now
It's the reassurance
Of your presence
That's championing
My reemergence.

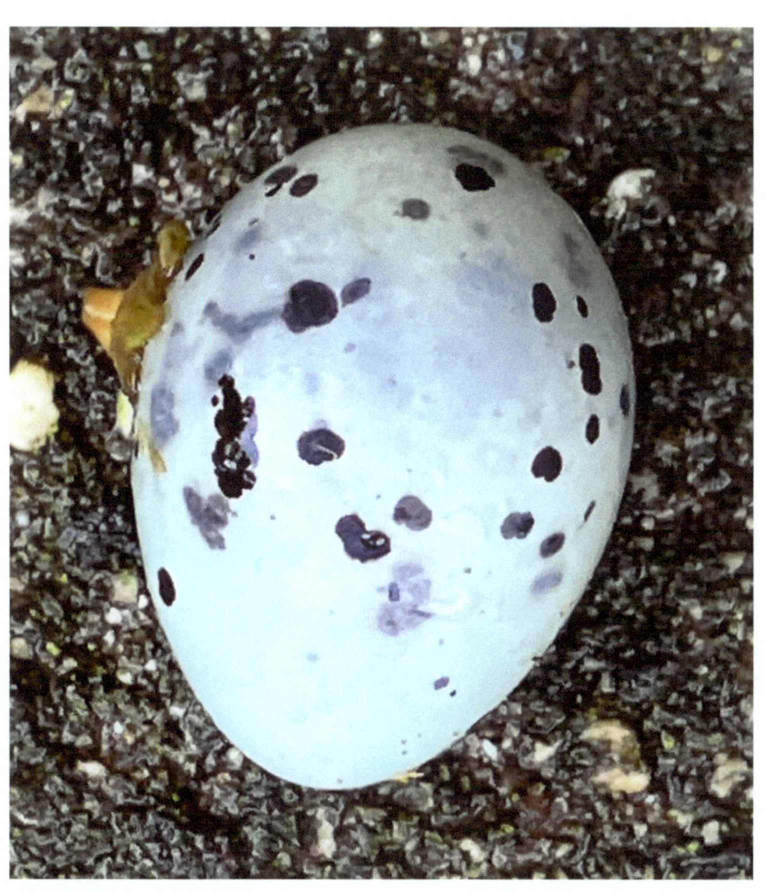

Breaking Free

The temporary haven
Of the cocoon
Must be broken
Because upon achieving
Magnificent transformation
The butterfly
Can no longer
Be confined
By what was.

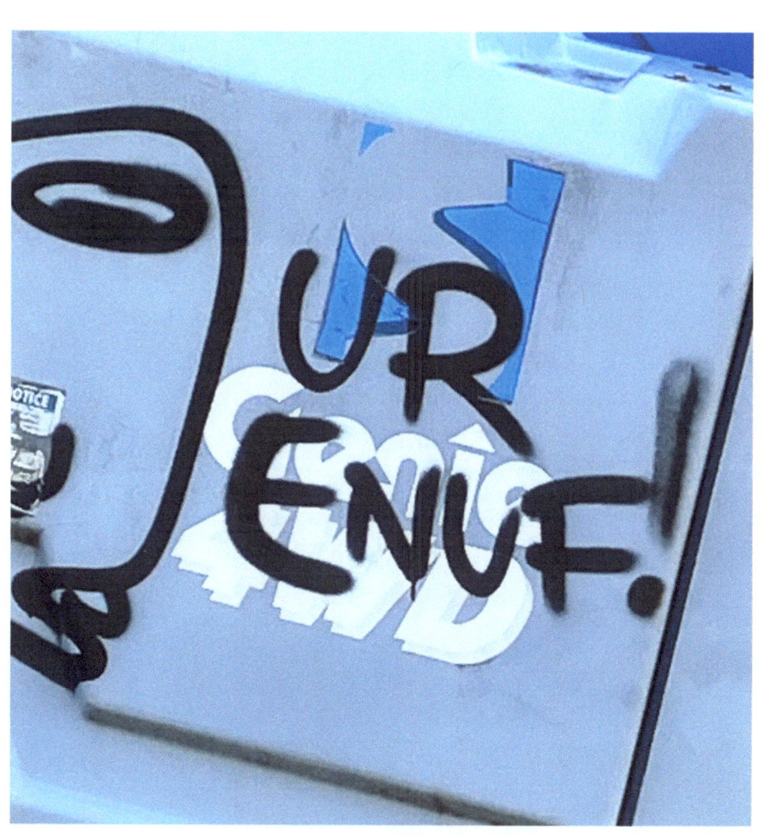
UR
ENUF!

I Don't

Do you promise
To remain the same
Mentally emotionally and physically
Forever?
Do you promise
To live small enough to fit
Within the life you've outgrown
Forever?
Do you promise
To plant your heart
In soil devoid of like or love
Forever?
I don't.

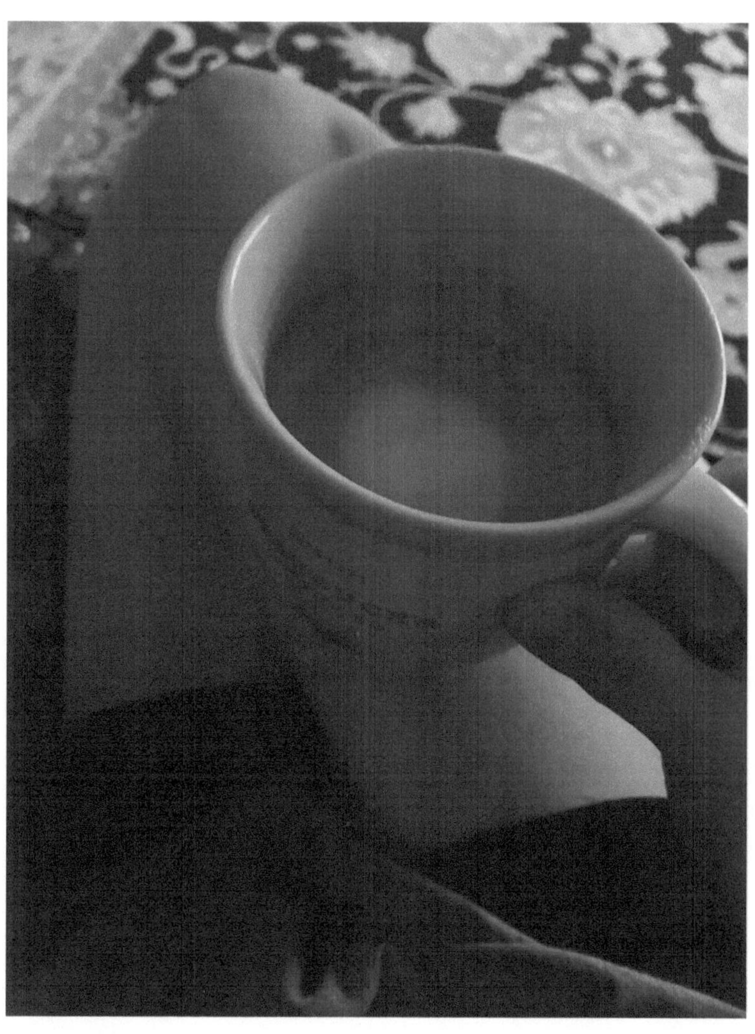

About the Author

Catherine Thomas is a speaker and host of *The Catherine Thomas Podcast* and *The Compassionate Conversation Series With Catherine Thomas*. *Inspiration From What Is* is her second collection of poetry and photography.

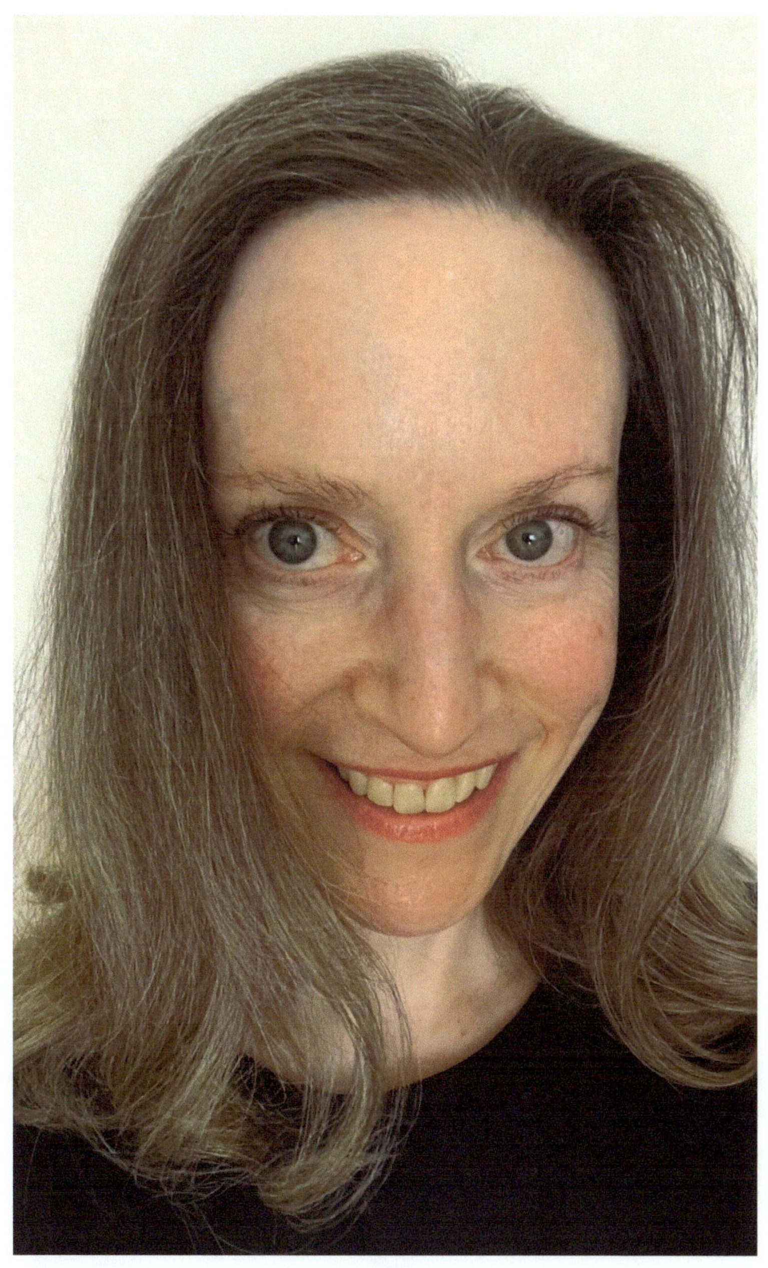

www.ingramcontent.com/pod-product-compliance
Lightning Source LLC
LaVergne TN
LVHW052250100826
845147LV00001B/7

* 9 7 9 8 2 1 8 4 6 5 6 8 1 *